DEUTSCH ALS FREMDSPRACHE NIVEAU A2/1

Schritte 3 international

Glossary XXL
Deutsch–Englisch
German–English

Hueber Verlag

English Translation and Adaption:
Jeannie Sanke

Authors:
Sophie Caesar (Familiarity and Understanding, Getting It All Down)
María Jesús Gil Valdés (Listening and Pronunciation)
Christiane Seuthe (Forms and Structures)
Wilfried Völker (Fragments of History)

Quellenverzeichnis
Fotos:
Seite 14: © Stadt Mainz, Amt für Öffentlichkeitsarbeit
Seite 15: © Sophie Caesar
Seite 24: © akg-images/Erich Lessing
Seite 25: oben: © Stuttgart-Marketing GmbH; unten: © Finest Images/Chromeorange
Seite 37: oben rechts: © irisblende.de; unten links: © Sophie Caesar
Seite 38: © irisblende.de
Seite 48: © Fraunhofer IPK, Stasi-Schnipsel-Projekt
Seite 49: alle: © courtesy of The University of Texas Libraries, The University of Texas at Austin
Seite 58/60/79: © panthermedia.net/Matthias. K.
Seite 59: © dpa Picture Alliance/Udo Bernhart
Seite 69: oben rechts: © VISUM/Goetz Schleser; unten links: © picture-alliance/akg-images
Seite 78: oben rechts: © picture-alliance/akg-images; unten links: © picture-alliance/ZB
Alle anderen Fotos und Umschlagfoto: Alexander Keller.

3. 2. 1. | Die letzten Ziffern
2013 12 11 10 09 | bezeichnen Zahl und Jahr des Druckes.
Alle Drucke dieser Auflage können, da unverändert,
nebeneinander benutzt werden.
1. Auflage

Zeichnungen: Jörg Saupe, Düsseldorf
Layout: Erwin Schmid, Hueber Verlag, Ismaning
Satz: Typosatz W. Namisla GmbH, München
Redaktion: CoLibris-Lektorat Dr. Barbara Welzel, Göttingen
Druck und Bindung: Ludwig Auer GmbH, Donauwörth
Printed in Germany
ISBN 978-3-19-451853-7

Preface

Dear Learner,

in this **XXL Glossary** you will find, as its title suggests, much more than just a glossary. Each chapter includes the following sections:

Vocabulary
All new words are presented in the order in which they appear in both the course book and the workbook, page-by-page, then alphabetically. Unlike a dictionary, this glossary allows you to learn words in context so that their meaning is far more real to you than a dictionary entry.

Forms and Structures
In this section, we explain grammar based on concrete examples from the course book and compare and contrast the structures with those of English. As the course proceeds, you will find continued reference in newer sections to material in previous chapters to help reinforce your understanding and mastery of these points. We also make a point of pointing out differences between English and German that can potentially hinder your understanding or lead you into traps.
We have also included additional **translation exercises** in each chapter to help you get a better sense of your progress and mastery, allowing you to see more how German and English are similar and different.

Listening and Pronunciation
As important as grammar, structure and vocabulary are, without knowing the sound system, they are of no use. In this section, we aim to give you the tools you will need not only to recognize the sounds of German, but to reproduce them so that you can be understood, even when your structural knowledge is weak.

Familiarity and Understanding
No language exists apart from the culture in which it is couched. Here you will learn about the German-speaking areas of the world, their literature and arts, and aspects of daily life. There is a good deal of history in this section, and we believe this will help you to understand a significant amount of contemporary culture and how it came to be as it is.

Self-Evaluation
At the end of each chapter, you have the opportunity to evaluate your progress on the objectives in each unit, allowing you to give extra attention and/or seek extra help in areas where you are not as confident in your new skills.

We hope that you find this volume helps you learn German with greater ease and more enjoyment, and we wish you every success.

Sincerely,

the authors and editors

Contents

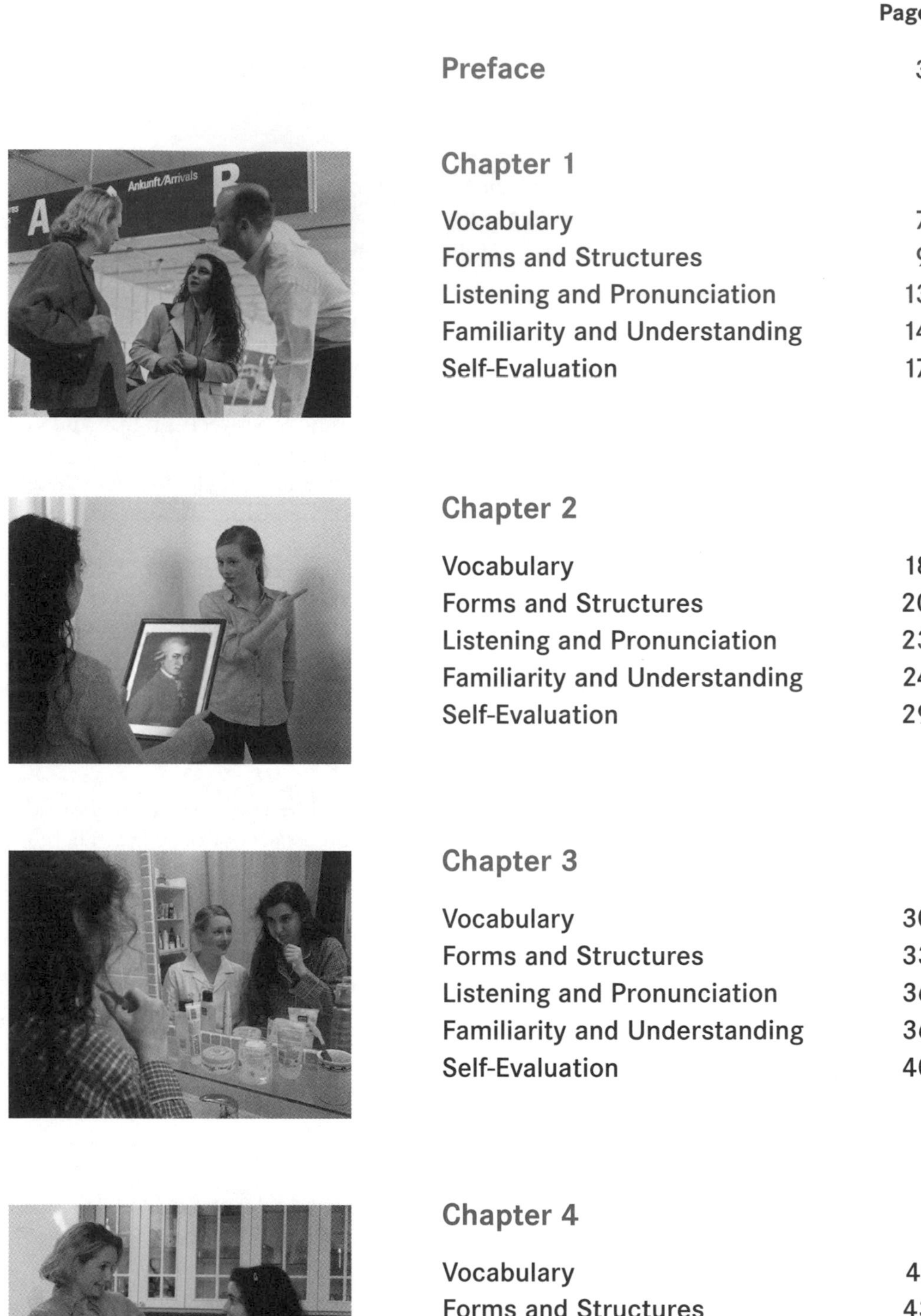

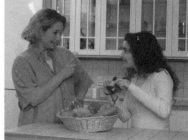

Contents

Vocabulary/Kursbuch

Die kursiv gedruckten Wörter werden in den Prüfungen Start Deutsch und Zertifikat Deutsch nicht verlangt.	Italicized words are not required for the examinations Start Deutsch or Zertifikat Deutsch.

Kursbuch — Textbook

Seite 7 — page 7

Seite 7	page 7
herum·gehen, er ist herumgegangen	*to go around, go around the circle*
das Instrument, -e	instrument
mehrere	several

Seite 8 — page 8

Seite 8	page 8
der/die Verwandte, -n	relative

Seite 9 — page 9

Seite 9	page 9
getrennt	separated
schwanger	pregnant
verpassen	to miss, arrive too late to catch
zusammen·leben	to live together

Seite 10 — page 10

Seite 10	page 10
die Ausrede, -n	*excuse*
eigentlich	actually, really
einzig	only, sole
essen gehen, er ist essen gegangen	to go out to eat
fröhlich	merry, jolly
die Geschäftsreise, -n	*business trip*
möglichst	as much/many as possible
traurig	sad
weil	because (subordinating conjunction)

Seite 11 — page 11

Seite 11	page 11
auf·hängen	*to hang up*
aus·packen	to unpack
ein·schlafen, er ist eingeschlafen	to fall asleep
das Mal, -e	time, turn
der Nachbar, -n / die Nachbarin, -nen	neighbor
öfters	fairly often, regularly
das Pech (nur Singular)	bad luck
peinlich	*embarrassing*
die Perfektform, -en	*present perfect form*
schließlich	finally
zurück·fahren, er ist zurückgefahren	to go back (by vehicle)

Seite 12 — page 12

Seite 12	page 12
acht·geben, du gibst acht, er gibt acht, er hat achtgegeben	to pay attention
auf einmal	all at once
der Autoschlüssel, –	car key
diskutieren	to discuss
erleben	to experience
erst einmal	for starters
die Flughafen-Polizei (nur Singular)	airport police
sich melden	to get in contact, be in contact
rein·spazieren	*to go walking in, strolling in*
schon einmal	once already
selbe	same
der Sitz, -e	seat
die Tasse, -n	cup
unbequem	*uncomfortable*
wenigstens	at least
der Zufall, ¨e	coincidence

Seite 13 — page 13

Seite 13	page 13
der Cousin, -s / die Cousine, -n	cousin
das Enkelkind, -er	grandchild
der Genitiv, -e	*genitive case*
der Neffe, -n	nephew
die *Nichte*, -n	*niece*
der Onkel, –	uncle
der Schwager, – / die Schwägerin, -nen	*brother-in-law, sister-in-law*
der Schwiegervater, ¨e	father-in-law
der Stammbaum, ¨e	*family tree*
die *Tante*, -n	aunt
die Verwandtschaft, -en	*relationship*

Seite 14 — page 14

Seite 14	page 14
allein erziehend	raising (a child) as a single parent
aus·gehen, er ist ausgegangen	to go out
die Dachwohnung, -en	*attic apartment*
ein·ziehen, er ist eingezogen	to move in
die Großfamilie, -n	*extended family*
die Hausarbeit (nur Singular)	*housework*
die Kleinfamilie, -n	*immediate family*
die Lebensform, -en	*way of life*
nebenan	next door
die Schwiegereltern (nur Plural)	parents-in-law
die Schwiegermutter, ¨e	mother-in-law
der Single, -s	*single person*
verwöhnen	*to spoil/pamper*

Vocabulary/Kursbuch

Seite 15	page 15
berichten	to report
das Erstaunen (nur Singular)	*amazement*
die Häufigkeit (nur Singular)	*frequency*
das Mitgefühl (nur Singular)	*sympathy*
das Präfix, -e	*prefix*
die Zeitabfolge, -n	*chronology, sequence of events*

Seite 16	page 16
der Fußballverein, -e	*football club*
der Hafen, ¨-e	port, harbor
das Kunstwerk, -e	*work of art*
nordostdeutsch	*northeast German*
die Ostsee (nur Singular)	*Baltic Sea*
die Partnerstadt, ¨-e	*sister city*
die Städtepartnerschaft, -en	*sister city relationship*
die Universitätsstadt, ¨-e	*university city, college town*

Seite 17	page 17
das Kennenlern-Lied, -er	*song about getting to know each other*
nach·singen, er hat nachgesungen	*to sing (in repetition)*
nordwestdeutsch	*northwest German*
die Städtefreundschaft, -en	*friendship between cities*
der Stadtname, -n	*city name*
zweitgrößte	second largest

Arbeitsbuch / Workbook

Seite 84	page 84
die Kinokarte, -n	movie theater ticket

Seite 86	page 86
schrecklich	frightening

Seite 87	page 87
die Pizzeria, Pizzerien	pizzeria

Seite 88	page 88
nach·schlagen, du schlägst nach, er schlägt nach, er hat nachgeschlagen	to look up (a reference)

Seite 89	page 89
kombinieren	*to combine*
packen	to pack

Seite 90	page 90
der/die Lieblingsverwandte, -n	*favorite relative*

Seite 91	page 91
das Chaos (nur Singular)	*chaos*
die Diskussion, -en	discussion
die Harmonie (nur Singular)	*harmony*
der Lieblingsjoghurt, -s	*favorite yogurt*
nonstop	*non-stop*
verwandt	related

1 The conjunction *weil* (Konjunktion)

examples

Susanne und Kurt brauchen ein Au-pair-Madchen.
*Das Baby **kommt** bald.*
Susanne und Kurt brauchen ein Au-pair-Mädchen,
***weil** das Baby bald **kommt**.*

Susanne and Kurt need an au pair.
The baby is due soon.
Susanne and Kurt need an au pair because
the baby is due soon.

*Franz ist sauer. Er **kann** das*
Fußballspiel nicht sehen.
*Franz ist sauer, **weil** er das*
*Fußballspiel nicht sehen **kann**.*

Franz is upset/angry. He can't see the
football game.
Franz is upset because he can't see the
football game.

The conjuntion *weil* introduces a subordinate clause that indicates the cause of the situation in the main clause. In subordinate clauses, the conjugated verb is not in second position, but in the final position. In German, main and subordinate clauses are always separated by a comma.

examples

Ich fahre nachts nicht gern Auto.
*Ich **schlafe** da immer **ein**.*

I don't like to drive at night.
I always fall asleep [then].

Ich fahre nachts nicht gern Auto,
***weil** ich da immer **einschlafe**.*

I don't like to drive at night because
I always fall asleep [then].

In subordinate clauses, verbs with separable prefixes always rejoin their prefixes in final position.

examples

***Warum** kommst du denn so spät?* — Why are you so late?

Weil ich den Bus verpasst habe. — Because I missed the bus.

The interrogative *warum?* is used to ask about the reason for or cause of something.
When answering a question with *warum?* it is acceptable to answer straight off with a subordinate clause beginning with *weil*, provided the intent of the main clause is understood (in this case, *Ich komme so spät, weil …*).

examples

Susanne und Kurt brauchen ein Au-pair-Mädchen,
***denn** das Baby **kommt** bald.*

Susanne and Kurt need an au pair
because the baby is due soon.

In *Schritte international 2*, Chapter 14, we looked at the causal conjunction denn. In contrast to *weil*, *denn* is a coordinating conjunction, meaning that it joins two main clauses. As such, the conjugated verb does not change position after *denn*; it stays in the second position. It must be noted, however, that a *warum?* question is never answered with *denn* but only with *weil*.

2 The perfect tense: separable verbs *(Perfekt: trennbare Verben)*

examples

*Ich **bin** gut zu Hause **angekommen**.*	I got home fine.
*Ich **habe** den Koffer gleich **ausgepackt**.*	I unpacked my suitcase straight away.
*Dann **habe ich** noch ein bisschen **ferngesehen**.*	Then, I watched a little TV.
*Ich **bin** schnell **eingeschlafen**.*	I fell asleep quickly.

Separable verbs (those consisting of a verb stem and a separable prefix) form the *Perfekt* in the same manner as verbs with no prefix, pairing a conjugated form of *haben* or *sein* and the past participle of the verb in question. The separable prefix precedes the *ge-*, and the rest of the participle is identical to the participle of the stem verb (*an-ge-kommen, aus-ge-packt, fern-ge-sehen*).

Remember that verbs which form the *Perfekt* with *sein* are those indicating change of location (such as *ankommen*) or of condition (such as *einschlafen*) and they cannot take a direct object (accusative complement).

Also remember that separable prefixes are always stressed in speaking, even in past participles (***ein**-ge-schlafen, **aus**-ge-packt*).

3 The perfect tense: inseparable verbs *(Perfekt: nicht trennbare Verben)*

examples

***Bekommst** du auch immer so viele E-Mails?*	Do you always get so many e-mails?
***Erklären** Sie mir bitte mal die Aufgabe.*	Explain the assignment to me, please.
*Ich **verstehe** das nicht.*	I don't understand that.

Like separable verbs, inseparable verbs also have prefixes (such as *be-, er-,* and *ver-*), but these cannot separate from the verb stem. In further contrast to separable verbs, inseparable prefixes are never stressed in speech; the stress stays where it is in the verb stem.

examples

***Hast** du die E-Mail **bekommen**?*	Did you get the e-mail?
*Er **hat** die Aufgabe **erklärt**.*	He explained the assignment.
*Ich **habe** das nicht **verstanden**.*	I didn't understand that.

Inseparable verbs form the *Perfekt* in the same manner as "simple" and separable verbs, except that there is no *-ge-*: *be-kommen, er-klärt, ver-standen*.

4 The perfect tense: verbs ending in *-ieren (Perfekt: Verben auf -ieren)*

examples

*Ich **habe** gerade mit Laura **telefoniert**.*	I just spoke with Laura on the phone.
*Was **ist** denn **passiert**?*	What happened?

Verbs ending in *-ieren* (such as *telefonieren, passieren, diskutieren,* etc.) do not have a *ge-* syllable in their participles, either.

5 Proper nouns in genitive case – *von* + dative *(Nomen im Genitiv – von + Dativ)*

examples

Das ist Julias Großmutter. / Das ist die Großmutter von Julia.	This is Julia's grandmother.
Das ist Toms Cousin. / Das ist der Cousin von Tom.	This is Tom's cousin.

The genitive case of proper nouns is used to express possession and is formed with an *s* on the end of the name but **without** an apostrophe. Unlike English, only proper names can use a final *s* to indicate possession.
The genitive case may be replaced with a construction using the preposition *von*, as the Romance languages do with the prepositions *de* and *di*. Remember that German *von* requires a dative object:
Das ist die Großmutter von meiner Freundin Julia. / Das ist der Cousin von meinem Freund Tom.

6 The locational preposition *bei* + dative *(Lokale Präposition: bei + Dativ)*

examples

*Die Großmutter ist **bei** ihrer Tochter eingezogen.*	The grandmother moved in with her daughter [into her daughter's home].
*Meine Freundin lebt noch **bei** ihren Eltern, aber sie ist oft **bei** ihrem Freund.*	My girlfriend still lives with her parents (at her parents' [house]), but she is often at her boyfriend's [house].
*Larissa lebt **mit** Kurt und Simon **zusammen**.*	Larissa lives (together) with Kurt and Simon.

In *Schritte international* 2, Chapter 11, we saw how the preposition *bei* indicates location at someone's home or at an institution when it is referred to by its proper name.
Bei always indicates location (in someone's home, where) while *mit* expresses accompaniment or companionship (together/along) and is often accompanied by the adverb *zusammen*.
Both *bei* and *mit* require dative objects.

7 Translate into English.

a *Warum hast du mich nicht angerufen?* ....?

– Weil ich deine Handynummer nicht ....

hatte. ....:

b *Julie arbeitet als Au-pair-Mädchen,* ....

denn sie spielt gern mit Kindern. ....:

c *Peter ist schon wieder im Unterricht* ....

eingeschlafen. ....:

– Wie peinlich! ....!

8 Translate into German.

a How was the trip? Tell me!	…… mal!
– It was terrible!	– Es …… !
– Why? What happened?	…… ?
– I almost missed the plane and then	– Ich habe ……
the suitcases didn't arrive.	und dann …… .
– What bad luck!	…… !
b Would you please explain the exercise	……
again?	…… nochmal …… ?
– I explained it already!	– …… doch schon …… !
– Yes, but we didn't understand it.	…… .
c My brother is already 30, but he still	……
lives with my parents.	…… .
– Doesn't he work?	…… ?
– Yes, but he doesn't earn much and	…… er verdient ……
apartments are really expensive.	…… .

9 Translate into German.

a Why aren't you coming along?	…… mit?
– Because I still have to unpack. And	…… noch …… .
then I have to shop.	Und …… .
b I didn't go work out today because	……
I was so tired.	…… so …… .
– Yeah, but you can't go on Wednes-	……
day either because it's Julia's birthday.	…… .
c My cousin lives in Berlin. Her name is	……
Francine and she's studying economics.	…… .
She lives in a shared apartment together	……
with two girls from Poland.	…… .

Listening and Pronunciation

Pronunciation of <e> and vocalized <r>

bezahlen ● *gefallen*

As we learned in Chapter 8 of *Schritte international 2*, an unstressed <e> is short and almost like and American "uh" – a shwa. The same sound occurs with the <e> in the prefixes *be-* and *ge-* .

verpassen ● *erleben* ● *zerbrechen*

In similar fashion, the <r> in unstressed, inseparable prefixes sounds similar to the vowel vocal <a> or the so-called "Boston R".

Syllabic stress of verbs ending in *-ieren*

passieren ● *passiert*
diskutieren ● *diskutiert*

Verbs ending in *-ieren*, always have their stress on the <ie> of *-ieren*, whether in present or perfect tense.

Stress of sentence elements

Ich muss unbedingt noch Blumen kaufen.
Weil meine Mutter Geburtstag hat.

In a spoken sentence, the element with the most important information gets the primary stress. Generally, such elements tend to be located at or near the end of the sentence.

auf dem Tisch, hinter der Tasche

In the case of a group of elements, consisting of a preposition + article + noun, the noun will get the primary stress.

Intonation of main and subordinate clauses

Warum bist du nach Deutschland gekommen? ↘

In *Schritte international 1* and *2*, we observed how, as a general rule, spoken statements intone downward at the end, as do questions with interrogatives (*W-Fragen*).

Gehen wir morgen wirklich joggen? ↗

In closed, yes/no questions that begin with a verb, the intonation rises at the end.

Ich lerne Deutsch, → *weil ich Freunde in Deutschland habe.* ↘

If a main clause is followed by a subordinating clause or vice versa, the first clause has a flat or ascending intonation.

Familiarity and Understanding

Sister cities / *Partnerstädte*

The first record of any sister city relationship in history is between Paderborn (Germany) and Le Mans (France), dating to the 9th century as an informal agreement. Since then, over 2500 communities from 169 countries around the globe have recognized sister city arrangements. Between the United States and Germany, there are about 170 sister city partnerships between American and German communities that have arisen since President Eisenhower established the Sister Cities Program in 1956. Some, like Chicago and Hamburg, are based upon shared demographics (both are cities of about 2 million inhabitants with ports, major commercial centers and lively cultural communities) while others, such as tiny New Harmony Indiana and Wiernsheim Germany, are based on historical ties (New Harmony was settled originally by immigrants from Wiernsheim).

Sister city arrangements can seek to foster greater cultural understanding, to strengthen historical or commercial ties, and even to build tourism.

A house of cards

Since 2007, the city of Braunschweig has had a castle, which it had not for the 60 years before. In 1944, Allied bombing raids destroyed 90% of the city, and among the casualties was the castle which lay half in ruins. The story of the Braunschweig castle's destruction and subsequent reconstruction provides an informative lesson in civic movements in recent German history.
In 1959, 14 years after the war, the castle ruins remained. The City Council ordered the remains removed and showed no interest in rebuilding what they considered to be an anachronistic reminder of a feudal era. Though many would have preferred to leave the ruins to wait for better days, they could only watch a part of their city's identity be cleared away. Political reality of the time, however, needed to address the immediate pressing needs for more housing rather than monuments to history. In place of the castle, the city erected a park, but even its name seemed to rub salt in some wounds: it was called the *Schlosspark.*
Braunschweig as it exists today typifies city architecture of those years: functional, unornamented, suitable for auto traffic, modern, but asthetically empty. As unappealing as this is to us today, in its time, it addressed the urgent need to provide roofs over millions of heads in the decades following the war, though today, so much functionality is more happily forgotten in architectural circles. Perhaps this is why, after 50 years, a movement to resurrect the castle appeared.

Not everyone supports the resurrection. Defenders of the *Schlosspark*, among others, oppose felling 255 trees. Others oppose the commercial interests involved: 130 new shops and 20 restaurants await consumers behind the terrace. There are 30,000 m^2 (almost 323,000 ft^2) of space, and only one-third of it is devoted to cultural interests: a public library, an archive, a civil registry and a castle museum. Environmentalists and traditional merchants from the area joined forces to protest what they view as threats to both their interests. Still, their efforts were for naught:

Braunschweig now has its castle, complete with a terrace, and even a quadriga (a statue of a chariot drawn by four horses) in the front. How the castle's surroundings will develop remains to be seen; for now, two statues will gaze, fixedly and perhaps a bit surprised, out over a charming little town with some 60 shops offering clothing made in China, quick pizzas, and, of course, a McDonalds.

All of this ado takes place in a city devoid of the tourist traffic needed to make it known, unlike the reconstruction of Berlin's *Stadtschloss.* Yet both cases shed light upon sociological and architectural issues of interest across Germany.

Historical Fragments

The German Question and the student revolts

The Vienna Congress of 1814–15 set a new European order following Napoleon's final defeat at Waterloo. For Germany, the most important outcome was the establishment of the *Deutscher Bund* (German Confederation) succeeding the Holy Roman Empire. Among the 39 member states, the two largest, Prussia and Austria, fought over control of the Confederation. A few decades later, Prussia won this power struggle, and within a few years, Prussia became a modern state in which serfdom was abolished, cities developed, compulsory military service was introduced and the military hierarchy was reformed.
Scholar Wilhelm von Humboldt (his brother Alexander traveled throughout South America and made important discoveries in biology, geography and geology) introduced critical educational reforms. He founded the University of Berlin (1810) and introduced teacher training along with the final examinations at the end of Gymnasium education which still exist today as the *Abitur* (see Chapter 6 of this volume). New economic policies, coupled with better, merit-based education, enabled Prussia's economic rise by targeting open markets, free trade and competetiveness.

In 1834, Prussia succeeded in uniting many of the German states within the *Deutscher Zollverein*, a customs union which ended tariffs between the petty states. This union enabled participating states to double their net incomes in just 10 years, an unprecedented result. The *Zollverein* also enable construction of a new transportation network: the train railways. In 1848, the rail network was double the size of France's and four times as large as Austria's (and the latter was weakening). These many economic and political successes paved the way for demands that a constitution and democratic reforms be enacted.

Students united in *Burschenschaften* (forerunners of American fraternities). They had fought against and defeated Napoleon and went on to fight for a constitution, freedom of the press and free assembly, as well as for equality under the law. One of these *Burschenschaften* donned the black, red and yellow colors, which would later become those of the 20th century democrats, and eventually, the German republic.
Metternich, the leader of the Conservatives in Austria, sought to suppress these uprisings and he succeeded: the press was censored, *Burschenschaften* were banned, and dissenters were forbidden to prac-

tice their professions. Revolts continued to arise, nevertheless; in 1830, following the revolt in Paris, revolutionaries stormed the Braunschweig castle, then the Frankfurt police headquarters in 1833, and in spite of demagogues' persecution, democratic forces continued to demand a constitution, voting rights, a modern legal system and, above all, a united Germany.

These developments forced the question: who ruled this union of states? Austria? Prussia? The latter preferred a smaller solution, one state under its mandate, and a separate Austrian state. Other voices called for a larger empire including both Prussia and Austria.
The revolt of March 1848 and the parliament held in Frankfurt am Main attempted to address this question again, but failed because the German princes, including the King of Prussia, did not want a functioning democracy. The revolution failed and it fell to Bismarck to settle the "German Question" with a "revolution from above".

Self-Evaluation

Getting Acquainted

When listening, I can understand (Hören)

- Information on the telephone: *„Da kann ich Ihnen unseren Schnupperkurs empfehlen. Der dauert drei Tage …"*
- Simple interviews about housing and lifestyles: *„Ich lebe allein, habe aber viele Freunde."*
- Short dialogues about the course of my day: *„Ich bin um 3 Uhr aufgestanden."*
- Simple song lyrics such as the lyrics of the *„Kennenlernen"* song

In written texts, I can understand (Lesen)

- Short texts in the form of an invitation: *„Lieber Paul, am Samstag werde ich 30 …"*
- Brief magazine articles on topics of current interest: *„Studie: Deutsche sind Freizeitweltmeister"*

I can produce the following oral structures (Sprechen)

- Give reasons for something: *„Ich bin nicht gekommen, weil …"*
- Tell about the circumstances of an occurrence: *„Ich habe einmal meinen Schlüssel verloren. Das war in Berlin …"*
- Talk about close relatives
- Tell how friends, neighbors and acquaintances live
- Tell about experiences while traveling
- Talk about different lifestyles

I can produce the following written texts (Schreiben)

- Short notes: *„Lieber Herr Bauer, Frau Breiter hat angerufen. Bitte rufen Sie sie zurück."*
- Short notes or e-mails responding to an invitation
- Postcards describing what happened on a trip: *„Lieber …, stell dir vor: Am Wochenende …"*

Kursbuch	Textbook
Seite 18	**page 18**
das Amt, ¨er	*here*: government office
der Container, –	container
der Hausmeister, –	buildling manager, property supervisor
das Mietshaus, ¨er	rental building
der Müll (nur Singular)	garbage
der Müllmann, ¨er	garbageman
die Mülltonne, -n	dumpster
nicht mehr	no more, no longer
die Ordnung (nur Singular)	order
das Plastik (nur Singular)	plastic
die Sauberkeit (nur Singular)	cleanliness
sorgen für	to care for, see to
trennen	to separate; *here*: to sort
weg·werfen, du wirfst weg, er wirft weg, er hat weggeworfen	to throw away, discard
werfen, du wirfst, er wirft, er hat geworfen	to throw

Seite 19	page 19
hängen	to hang
der Hof, ¨e	*here*: courtyard
der Komponist, -en	*composer*
der Lieblingskomponist, -en	*favorite composer*
die Spanierin, -nen	*Spaniard (female)*
Südamerika (nur Singular)	*South America*

Seite 20	page 20
der Boden, ¨	floor
die Decke, -n	*here:* ceiling
erstellen	*to produce, generate*
der Müllcontainer, –	*waste container*
stecken	*here*: to be within
der Teppich, -e	rug
die Wiederholung, -en	*here: review*

Seite 21	page 21
an·schauen	to look at
die Decke, -n	ceiling
der Hausschuh, -e	house shoe, slipper
legen (sich)	to lay/put (oneself) in a reclining position
die Rolle, -n	role
die Schublade, -n	*drawer*
das Schuhregal, -e	shoe shelf
tauschen	*to exchange*
der Turnschuh, -e	*gym shoe, sneaker*
verlassen, du verlässt, er verlässt, er hat verlassen	to leave, abandon
verstecken	to conceal, hide

Seite 22	page 22
der Kleiderschrank, ¨e	wardrobe (furniture)
rauf	*up top*
raus	*out*
raus·kommen	*to come out*
rein	*in, inside (directional)*
rüber	*over (there)*
runter	*under (there)*

Seite 23	page 23
ab·stellen	to put away
der Aufzug, ¨e	elevator
das Aussehen (nur Singular)	appearance (how one looks)
bereits	*already*
beruflich	*professionally, in the course of one's work*
flüstern	*to whisper*
der Hochzeitstag, -e	*wedding day*
der Kinderwagen, –	stroller, pram
die Kiste, -n	crate
küssen (sich)	to kiss (each other)
der Mieter, –	*renter*
still	silent
streiten (sich), er hat (sich) gestritten	to argue (with each other)
der Tratsch (nur Singular)	*gossip*
tratschen	*to gossip*

Seite 24	page 24
an sein, es ist an, es ist an gewesen	to be [turned] on
ärgerlich	aggravating
aus·leihen, er hat ausgeliehen	*here: to borrow*
aus·stellen	to exhibit
bedanken (sich)	to thank
Bescheid sagen	to give information
bis dann	till then
der Briefkasten, ¨	mailbox
furchtbar	frightening, awful
gießen, er hat gegossen	*to pour*
die Langschläferin, -nen	*woman who sleeps a long time*
der Mitbewohner, –	*roommate (male)*
die Mitbewohnerin, -nen	*roommate (female)*
die Pflanze, -n	plant
sauber machen	to clean
die Stromrechnung, -en	electric bill
verbrauchen	to use
wahnsinnig	crazy, nutty, insane
wecken	to wake
die WG, -s	*apartment shared by multiple residents*

Seite 25 / page 25

Seite 25	page 25
der Ärger (nur Singular)	aggravation
das Bedauern (nur Singular)	*regret*
das Direktional-Adverb, -ien	*directional adverb*
die Grußformel, -n	*form of greeting*
die Hoffnung, -en	hope
runter·kommen, er ist runtergekommen	*to come down*
die Wechselpräposition, -en	*preposition that can take objects in either accusative or dative case*

Seite 26 / page 26

Seite 26	page 26
die Attraktion, -en	*attraction*
außen	outside
bauen	to build
der Bezirk, -e	*district, precinct*
bunt	multicolored
das Dach, ⸚er	roof
kunsthistorisch	*art historic*
der Künstler, –	artist
die Linie, -n	line
nicht nur	not only
das Originalzitat, -e	*original quotation/citation*
das Quiz, -e	quiz
das Riesenrad, ⸚er	*Ferris wheel*
das Wohnhaus, ⸚er	*apartment building*

Seite 27 / page 27

Seite 27	page 27
alternativ	alternative
Asien	*Asia*
der Bau, Bauten	construction
die Baukosten (nur Plural)	*construction costs*
die Bauzeit, -en	*construction time*
die Dachterrasse, -n	*roof terrace*
der Eigentümer, –	*owner*
entwickeln	to develop
die Erde (nur Singular)	earth, soil
der Fakt, -en	*fact*
der Gemeinschaftsraum, ⸚e	*common room*
die Gesamtnutzfläche, -n	*total usuable space*
der Geschäftsraum, ⸚e	*business space*
der Kinderspielplatz, ⸚e	*play area for children*
die Kunst, ⸚e	art
der Pazifische Ozean (nur Singular)	*Pacific Ocean*
der Philosoph, -en	*philosopher*
planen	to plan
der Raum, ⸚e	space
die Studienreise, -n	*study trip*
t (die Tonne, -n)	*ton (unit of weight); 1 metric ton = 2.2 English tons*
unmenschlich	*inhuman*
verändern (sich)	to change, alter (oneself)
der Wintergarten, ⸚	*winter garden*

Arbeitsbuch / Workbook

Seite 94 / page 94

Seite 94	page 94
der Papierkorb, ⸚e	*wastepaper basket*

Seite 97 / page 97

Seite 97	page 97
die Schreibtischlampe, -n	desk lamp

Seite 98 / page 98

Seite 98	page 98
rauf·fahren, du fährst rauf, er fährt rauf, er ist raufgefahren	*to travel up, go up*
rauf·gehen, er ist raufgegangen	*to go up (on foot)*
rein·gehen, er ist reingegangen	*to go in (on foot)*
rüber·gehen, er ist rübergegangen	*to go over (on foot)*
runter·fahren, du fährst runter, er fährt runter, er ist runtergefahren	*to travel down, go down*

Seite 100 / page 100

Seite 100	page 100
der Fahrradkeller, –	*bicycle cellar*
das Gartenhaus, ⸚er	*garden house*
die Mietwohnung, -en	*rental apartment*

Seite 101 / page 101

Seite 101	page 101
weg·gehen, er ist weggegangen	to go away

Seite 102 / page 102

Seite 102	page 102
die Richtungsangabe, -n	*indication of travel direction*

1 Two-way prepositions *(Wechselpräpositionen)*

examples

***Wo** ist denn das Wörterbuch?*	**Where's** the dictionary?
(Das ist) ***im*** *Regal. /*	(It's) **on** the bookshelf. /
auf dem *Schreibtisch. /*	**on** the desk. /
neben den *Lexika.*	**next to** the encyclopedias.

In Chapter 11 of *Schritte international 2,* we saw that the locational prepositions *an, auf, hinter, in, neben, unter, über, vor* and *zwischen*, combined with a dative object, indicate a location or an answer to the question *wo?*

examples

***Wohin** kommt denn das Wörterbuch?*	**Where** does the dictionary go [to]?
(Das kommt) ***ins*** *Regal. /*	(That goes) **on[to]** the bookshelf. /
auf den *Schreibtisch. /*	**on[to]** the desk. /
neben die *Lexika.*	**next to** the encyclopedias.

When these same prepositions answer the question *wohin?* indicating destination of movement, they take accusative objects. We do not often differentiate between location and destination in English, but it is inescapable in German. Note in the examples above, in some cases, we sometimes have the option of adding "-to" onto the preposition to show movement toward a point. In English, this is optional and growing more infrequent. German **always** differentiates between location and destination, and with these nine prepositions, the case of the object depends upon which condition applies. For this reason, they are known as "two-way" prepositions.

2 Verbs used with two-way prepositions *(Verben mit Wechselpräpositionen)*

examples

***Wo** ist denn mein Handy?*	Where's my cell phone?
Das ***liegt*** *da auf dem Tisch.*	It's (lying) there on the table.
Wo sind denn die Autoschlüssel?	Where are my car keys?
Die ***stecken*** *bestimmt in deiner Jacke.*	They're hiding in your jacket for sure.
Wo ist denn das neue Poster?	Where's the new poster?
Das ***hängt*** *schon in der Klasse.*	It's already (hanging) in the classroom.
Wo sind denn die XXL-Glossare?	Where are the XXL glossaries?
Die ***stehen*** *da im Regal.*	They're (standing) on the shelf there.
Wo bist du denn jetzt?	Where are you right now?
Ich ***sitze*** *im Bus.*	I'm (sitting) on the bus.

In Chapter 11 of *Schritte international 2,* we also gained some familiarity with the verbs that accompany two-way prepositions and how some of them can and often do replace *sein* when describing the location of someone or something.

Remember: the verb *liegen* generally indicates a horizontal, reclining position, as opposed to *stehen*, which indicates a vertical orientation.
It is a very good idea to closely note the contexts in which these verbs appear, since most of them will not come naturally to native speakers of English.

stecken	*hat gesteckt*
hängen	*hat gehangen*
liegen	*hat/ist gelegen*
stehen	*hat/ist gestanden*
sitzen	*hat/ist gesessen*

Except for the verb *stecken*, every one of these verbs is irregular and forms its past participle with *-en*. Some of them form the *Perfekt* with *sein* and some with *haben*: formation with *sein*, however, is only heard or seen in southern Germany and in Austria.

examples

Wohin *soll ich denn das Handy legen?* ***Leg*** *es bitte auf den Tisch.*	Where should I put the cell phone? Put it on the table, please.
Wohin kommen denn die Autoschlüssel? ***Steck*** *sie bitte in meine Jacke.*	Where do the car keys go? Put them in my jacket, please.
Wohin kommt denn das neue Poster? ***Häng*** *es doch schon in die Klasse.*	Where does the new poster go? Go ahead and hang it up in the classroom.
Wohin kommen denn die XXL-Glossare? ***Stell*** *sie doch da ins Regal.*	Where do the XXL glossaries go? Go ahead and put them on the shelf there.
Wohin willst du die neue Schülerin ***setzen****?* *Die setzen wir neben Monika.*	Where do you want to put (seat) the new student? We'll put (seat) her next to Monika.

When describing destination and not location, the verbs *liegen*, *stehen* and *sitzen* are replaced by *legen*, *stellen* and *setzen*. The verbs *stecken* and *hängen* are used for both location and destination, but note that *hängen* is different in the past tense, as indicated in the list of participles below. Again, when describing destination, the object of the preposition is accusative. Look also at the fact that all of the verbs that accompany *wohin?* are transitive; they also take accusative complements. So do not be confused by the fact that the verbs have accusative objects and the prepositions also have accusative objects, all in the same sentence.

As opposed to verbs of location, verbs of destination are all weak:

stecken	*hat gesteckt*
hängen	*hat gehängt*
legen	*hat gelegt*
stellen	*hat gestellt*
setzen	*hat gesetzt*

examples

Wohin *soll ich die Blumen stellen?*	=	***Wo*** *soll ich die Blumen* ***hin****stellen?*
Wohin *hast du das Geld gelegt?*	=	***Wo*** *hast du das Geld* ***hin****gelegt?*
Wohin *kommt denn das Wörterbuch?*	=	***Wo*** *kommt denn das Wörterbuch* ***hin****?*

In spoken languages, very often the syllable *hin* will separate from *wo* and attach to the verb like a prefix. There is no change in meaning; it is the same as *wohin*.

3 Directional adverbs *(Direktionaladverbien)*

*Fahren Sie hier den Berg **rauf**.*	Drive up the mountain here.
*Ich bringe mal den Müll **runter**.*	I'll bring the garbage down.
*Kommt ihr **rüber** zu uns?*	Are you all coming over to our house?
*Möchten Sie nicht **reinkommen**?*	Wouldn't you like to come in?
*Gehst du bitte mit dem Hund **raus**?*	Would you please go out with the dog?

The directional adverbs *rauf* (up[wards]), *rüber* (over [to another point]), *runter* (down[wards]), *rein* (in[wards]) and *raus* (out[wards]) are used primarily in spoken language and are dependent upon the point of view of the speaker (where s/he is located in relation to the action). They combine with verbs of motion such as *bringen, gehen kommen, fahren*, and so on, and form separable verbs.

4 Translate into English.

a *Wo sind denn die Müllcontainer?* ....?

– Die stehen unten im Hof. ....:

b *Ich finde meine Schlüssel nicht.* ....:

– Du hast sie doch auf den Tisch gelegt. ....:

c *Stell das Fahrrad doch hinter das Haus.* ....:

– Ach nein, ich bringe es lieber in den Keller. ....
....:

d *Die Flaschen gehören hier rein und das Papier kommt da hin.* ....
....:

– Und wohin kommt der Plastikmüll? ....?

e *Kommt ihr rüber? Wir können jetzt essen.* ....:

– Warte, wir kommen gleich. ....:

5 Translate into German.

a Have you seen my cell phone? ....?

– Yeah, you put in in your jacket. ....:

b Ms. Söll, where did you put the CD-ROM? ....
....?

– It's lying on your desk. ....:

c Here, put the photos in the desk. *Hier,* ....:

– No, I want to hang them on the wall. ....:

6 Summarize in German.

A colleague from work left you the following note. Your intern from Austria does not understand it. Summarize it in German for him.

I need someone to reserve a single room in the name of Peter Gomez for two nights.
While you're at it, call the Tourist Information Center. I want to organize a guided tour.
And please also get two tickets for the theater tomorrow.
Thanks a lot,
Frank

Wir .... ein ....

und ....

Listening and Pronunciation

Pronunciation of <e>, <ö>, <i> and <ü>

lesen ● *lösen*

The difference between <e> and <ö> rests upon the lips; to create <ö>, the lips must be rounded as an "o". The <e> has no rounding.
We have no equivalent for the <ö> vowel, and in speech, Americans tend to pronounce it as though it were an <ur>, but there is no <r> sound. Pushing the tongue forward in your mouth, away from the throat, will help avoid this tendency.

Fliegen ● *Flüge*

The vowel <ü> is another problematic sound for English speakers. Again, rounding the lips to the shape of the <u> sound while saying <i> in the mouth will create the sound.

Syllabic stress in compound words

Hausnummer
Dachwohnung

As a general rule, the first part of a compound noun is the part that carries the primary stress. This coincides with the first part usually providing the most important information within the word.

Familiarity and Understanding

Bauhaus: the reinvention of the everyday

There are items which man has created that have not changed substantially from their invention onward. Some examples are books, chairs and forks.

However, there was a time, in the 19th century, in the wake of industrialization, when certain artists demanded that every spoon, pitcher, table, bed or chair should be reinvented. They were critical of industrial mass production and wanted to encourage handicrafts. This movement emerged in England and soon spread to architects and artists in Germany. Berlin came into the design and architecture movement of the *Werkbund* at the beginning of the 20th century, working according to practically ethical principles: the adequacy of the material and an object's functionality, purity and sustainability were what mattered above all else.
The *Werkbund* wanted to establish a new aesthetics of art, a new handicraft industry and new forms, more pure than those that had existed thus far.

One could say that this school of art was the predecessor of the *Bauhaus* school which sought an even deeper reform: to eliminate the differences between the artist and the craftsman. Its director-founder Walter Gropius wanted independent artists of all kinds together at the school.

According to Gropius, construction and architectural foundation were also works of art, as they joined all forms of artistic expression and craft. As an architect, Gropius built industrial buildings and housing blocks, among others. As a designer, he planned interior wallpaper, furniture and even a locomotive.

The *Bauhaus* School was created to train artists and artisans in the craft of art and was free to both academics and for those who did not follow the open philosophy of its founders and teachers. The departments allowed students to learn design, ceramics, textiles, typography, binding or working with glass, among others. Students received training prior to classes in which they learned to deal with different materials as well as the properties of colors and shapes. Among the more celebrated students and members of the school were Swiss artist Paul Klee (bookbinding classes), American Lyonel Feininger (printing classes) and the Russian Vassily Kandinski (mural painting). Many objects that the *Bauhaus* school invented, amended or modified led to industrial prototypes. Even today, many furniture items, lamps, games and cooking utensils still embody classic *Bauhaus* designs.

In 1930, Ludwig Mies van der Rohe joined the *Bauhaus* School as both its director and as an architect. Mies van der Rohe's architecture is well known in the United States; though his entry in the Chicago Tribune Tower competition was not chosen, he did design the iconic IBM and IIT buildings in Chicago, joining a collection of architectural examples perhaps unparalleled elsewhere. He is also known for the Martin Luther King Jr. Museum in Washington DC and the CN Tower in Toronto.

Achitecture for every taste: the 1920s and 30s

In 1927, Ludwig Mies van der Rohe and other architects under his leadership designed an entire neighborhood in the hills of Stuttgart, the *Weißenhofsiedlung*, which still stands. Even today, is considered a model of modern suburban design. Almost all the houses have roof terraces, and the construction is functional yet still boast's beautiful proportions. The 21 buildings containing 63 apartments are still considered an icon of avant-garde architecture.

This did not always remain so: during the Nazi era, the *Weißenhofsiedlung* was maligned as an Arab village (a most disparaging appellation), due to its predominant white color and the roof terraces. After only 10 years, the development was set to be demolished. Curiously, the Second World War, as devastating as it was to German cities, ended up saving the *Weißenhofsiedlung* from destruction, as the Nazis became distracted by other priorities.

In spite of some damages sustained in the Second World War, the *Weißenhofsiedlung* still stands, as does the *Kochenhofsiedlung* closer to the city center. Its construction is neither completely traditional nor experimental, but instead is best known for one unmistakable ingredient of popular German contemporary architecture: the so-called *Satteldach* or double-pitched roof on single-family homes. The dominant construction material of the settlement was traditional timber. As the *Weißenhofsiedlung* had his derogatory nickname, so did the *Kochenhofsiedlung*: to this day it is known as the *Holzwurmsiedlung* (woodworm settlement).

Whose work?

In 2006, a massive projected was completed, the new Berlin main train station. No sooner was it completed than a heated controversy erupted: instead of remaining true to the plans of the architect Gerkan, the *Deutsche Bahn* (German Rail) constructed a completely different ceiling than the vaulted one Gerkan had designed. Following this imbroglio, a raging debate ensued over intellectual property law. Does an architect's work belong to the architect or to the builder who realizes it?

Dear neighbors...

In *Stufen international 1 Glossary XXL* (Chapter 4), we mentioned that home ownership is not as much a priority for Germans as for Americans, and that there is no "renter's mentality" as we know it. Following this, and in stark contrast to life in the United States, courtesy among neighbors in apartment buildings as well as in single-family home neighborhoods is laid out in clear regulations.

Here are some of those rules which Germans are familiar with but which for foreigners might come as a surprise:

Noise

Neighbors are responsible, in as far as they are able, to avoid making noise in the house, common areas, patio and balcony. Special care should be taken at the following times: from 13:00 to 15:00 and 22:00 to 6:00 the next morning.
Music volume should be turned down to an unobtrusive level, and neighbors should be given advance notice of any parties being planned within the building.
It is forbidden to play any musical instrument during children's resting times — after lunch (13:00 to 15:00) — and from 19:00 to 8:00 the next morning. During other times, effort should be made to not play music for more than two consecutive hours.

Children

The maintenance and cleaning of the play area and the sandbox is the responsibility of parents whose children use the same. Children also have the responsibility to keep this area clean. Parents should be sure to retrieve their children's toys from these areas once play has ended.

Safety

Charcoal grilling on balconies is prohibited except in zones authorized by the community.

Housekeeping

- Garbage must be deposited in the appropriate containers. It must be properly separated into the appropriate containers for recycling and disposal. Old furniture, appliances and other items may not be deposited in these containers. The removal of these items is scheduled at regular intervals by local authorities (such collections are known as *Sperrmüll*).
- Flower and plant pots must be secured on windowsills. Care must be taken to keep water from dropping onto the wall beneath the windows or onto balconies or other neighbors.

Vehicles

• Motorized vehicles may not be parked in the courtyard, on sidewalks or in parks.
It is also forbidden to wash cars, change oil or carry out any repairs to them in the areas mentioned.
• Only bicycles may be parked in authorized areas in the basement within the appropriate space.

Pets

Domestic animals must be kept out of stairwells, outdoor areas or other common areas when not accompanied by their owners. Owners must ensure immediate removal of pets' waste, as well as keeping pets away from children's play areas.

Historical Fragments

The German National Anthem

Following the Napoleonic Wars, one of the new states in central Europe was given the name *Deutscher Bund* (German Federation). This Federation consisted of 39 individual states with no common head of state, no administration and no single common legislation, no common currency or customs authority and no unified army. Still, there existed throughout the Federation censorship and political persecution of the so-called demagogues who in turn demanded democracy and, above all, a legislative basis for a common form of government, a constitution. Liberal intellectuals demanded the creation of a single "German Nation."

A writer who was on vacation on the island of Helgoland in August 1841, an island in the North Sea which at that time had belonged to Britain since 1807, composed a "song of the Germans" (the *Deutschlandlied*), which in its third stanza summarized the Democrats' desires:

Einigkeit und Recht und Freiheit
Für das deutsche Vaterland!
Danach lasst uns alle streben
Brüderlich mit Herz und Hand!
Einigkeit und Recht und Freiheit
Sind des Glückes Unterpfand;
Blüh im Glanze dieses Glückes,
Blühe, Deutsches Vaterland.

Unity and justice and freedom
For the German fatherland!
Let us all strive for this
Brotherly with heart and hand.
Unity and justice and freedom
Are the pledge for happiness;
Blossom in the glory of this blessing,
Blossom, German fatherland.

The author had in mind the melody of "Ode to the Emperor" which Joseph Haydn had composed in 1797 in Vienna, in response to the French "Marseillaise". The author of the *Deutschlandlied* (Song of Germany), August Heinrich Hoffmann von Fallersleben (1798–1874), could not make a living from the success of his work, as during his lifetime he achieved no great degree of popularity.
In 1890, when the island of Helgoland was integrated into Germany, the song was sung during the official transfer of the island. Thus it became known and soon became one of the popular songs at that time.
This could have been due to the first words of the first stanza:

Deutschland, Deutschland über alles,
Über alles in der Welt ...

Germany, Germany above everything,
above everything in the world ...

The author claimed that, with this stanza, he was calling for German unity to reign over the small, individual German states. But soon this stanza was sung with euphoria by nationalists, and in the aftermath of First World War, the song left a very bad taste in many mouths.

In 1922, Friedrich Ebert, the first President of the first democratic republic in Germany (the Weimar Republic), proclaimed this song the "German National Anthem." For him, the third stanza in particular was significant.
After rising to power in 1933, the Nazis perverted the anthem for their own ends and allowed the first strophe to be sung. Against the backdrop of the Nazi's criminal policy of war, destruction and annihilation, the song evoked feelings of racism, megalomania and designs on world power. For that reason, the victorious Allies banned the national anthem in 1945. The first President of the Federal Republic of Germany after the war, founded in 1949, did compose a new anthem but it was not accepted.

In 1952, it was agreed to sing only the third stanza of the anthem as the *Deutschlandlied*. This agreement also held in 1990, following the reunification of the two German states.

Self-Evaluation

At home

	😃	🙂	😐
When listening, I can understand (Hören)			
– Simple instructions on where to place objects: *„Stell deine CDs ins Regal!"*			
– Conversations about other people: *„Du, über den habe ich schon ein paar Dinge gehört."*			
In written texts, I can understand (Lesen)			
– Informative notes or cards from others: *„Hallo Kathrin, du mein Fahrrad ist kaputt …"*			
– Short informational texts for tourists: *„Die Stadt Wien hat das Haus nach einer Idee des Wiener Künstlers …"*			
– Longer conversations, using listening strategies			
I can produce the following oral structures (Sprechen)			
– Name an object's or a person's location			
– Give directions			
I can produce the following written texts (Schreiben)			
– Small informative notes or cards asking someone for help: *„Liebe/r… Könntest du bitte einkaufen gehen? Ich habe keine Zeit …"*			
– Excusing myself: *„Lieber…, es tut mir wirklich sehr leid …"*			

Kursbuch	Textbook

Seite 28 — page 28

Seite 28	page 28
wach	awake

Seite 29 — page 29

Seite 29	page 29
dauernd	continually
erstaunt	*astounded*
der Frühstückstisch, -e	*breakfast table*
hart	hard (*here*: hard-boiled)
komisch	funny, odd, strange
die Nussschnecke, -n	*cinnamon bun with nuts*
die Sache, -n	thing
sonntags	Sundays
die Zitrone, -n	lemon

Seite 30 — page 30

Seite 30	page 30
ab und zu	now and then
allerdings	*here:* but I have to say, however
der Bettelmann, ¨er	*beggar, beggarman*
die Brezel, -n	*pretzel*
die Brotsorte, -n	*type of bread*
die Cornflakes (nur Plural)	*corn flakes*
das Croissant, -s	*croissant, French crescent roll*
drinnen	inside
duschen (sich)	to take a shower
eher	*rather, more*
ehrlich	honest
frisch	fresh
das Frühstücksinterview, -s	*breakfast interview*
der Gott, ¨er	god, God
Gott sei Dank	thank God
herzhaft	*hearty*
der Honig (nur Singular)	honey
im Sitzen	*while sitting*
im Stehen	*while standing*
der Kaiser, –	*kaiser, emperor*
die Marmelade, -n	marmelade
meistens	mostly
mittags	middays
pressen	*to squeeze, express (as in juice)*
selten	seldom, rarely
stundenlang	for hours
der Toast, -s	*toast, verbal dedication before drinking*
das Vitamin, -e	*vitamin*
werktags	workdays
das Wochenendfrühstück, -e	*weekend breakfast*
wochentags	weekdays
zusammen·sitzen, sie sind zusammengesessen	*to sit together*

Seite 31 — page 31

Seite 31	page 31
der Bierkrug, ¨e	*beer stein*
der Esslöffel, –	*tablespoon*
die Gabel, -n	fork
gewinnen, er hat gewonnen	to win
die Kanne, -n	coffee- or teapot
das Küchen-Quartett, -s	*kitchen quartet*
der Löffel, –	spoon
das Messer, –	knife
die Mikrowelle, -n	*microwave (oven)*
die Pfanne, -n	*pan (frying or saute)*
das Quartett, -e	*quartet*
die Quartettkarte, -n	*quartet ticket*
der Spieler, –	*player (male)*
die Spielerin, -nen	*player (female)*
der Teelöffel, –	*teaspoon*
der Topf, ¨e	pot
verteilen	*to divide up, distribute*
das Vollkornbrot, -e	*very dense, whole grain bread*

Seite 32 — page 32

Seite 32	page 32
besetzt	*here:* occupied, taken
drin sein, er ist drin, ist drin gewesen	*to be in*
das Gericht, -e	dish, entrée
der Kellner, –	waiter
die Kürbiscremesuppe, -n	*pumpkin crème soup*
der Latte Macchiato	*latte macchiato*
die Nudelsuppe, -n	noodle soup
Platz: Platz nehmen, du nimmst Platz, er nimmt Platz, hat Platz genommen	*here:* seat; to take a seat
die Portion, -en	portion
reklamieren	*to register a complaint*
der Rinderbraten, –	beef roast
der Schweinebraten, –	pork roast
setzen (sich)	to sit down
der Sitzplatz, ¨e	seat, place to sit
das Trinkgeld, -er	tip for restaurant or bar service
verzeihen, er hat verziehen	to forgive

Seite 33 — page 33

Seite 33	page 33
der Ausschnitt, -e	*excerpt*
beschäftigen (sich)	to occupy (oneself), keep busy
das Bohnengericht, -e	*bean dish*
braten, du brätst, er brät, er hat gebraten	to roast or fry
der Bundeskanzler, –	Chancellor (of the German Federation)
der Cheeseburger, –	*cheeseburger*
das Chili con carne (nur Singular)	*chili con carne (chili with meat)*
das Currypulver, –	*curry powder*
die Currywurst, ¨e	*curry wurst (bratwurst with a curry ketchup sauce)*
dagegen	*here: in contrast*
darüber	over that

dazu	*here: along with that*
ehemalig	*former*
das Fast Food (nur Singular)	*fast food*
fett	fat, greasy
die Fleischerei, -en	butcher shop
der Hamburger, –	*hamburger*
her·stellen	to manufacture
himmlisch	*heavenly*
die Imbissbude, -n	*snack vendor's stand*
das Jahrzehnt, -e	*decade*
der Kanzler, –	*chancellor*
das Ketchup (nur Singular)	*ketchup, catsup*
Lateinamerika	*Latin America*
die Lieblingsspeise, -n	*favorite dish*
die Mahlzeit, -en	mealtime
die Metzgerei, -en	butcher shop
nirgends	nowhere
der Popsänger, –	*pop singer*
probieren	to try, sample
raffiniert	*refined*
der Regierungschef, -s	head of government
das Rezept, -e	*here:* recipe
das Salamibrötchen, –	*salami sandwich (open-faced)*
salzig	*salty*
das Sandwich, -es	*sandwich*
das Sauerkraut (nur Singular)	*sauerkraut*
scharf	*here:* spicy, hot
das Schinkenbrötchen, –	ham sandwich
der Song, -s	*song*
die Sorte, -n	*sort, type*
süß	sweet
traditionell	*traditional*
typisch	typical
widmen	*to dedicate*
die Wurstart, -en	*type of sausage*
die Zeile, -n	line (of text)

Seite 34 — page 34

auf·essen, du isst auf, er isst auf, er hat aufgegessen	*to eat up*
die Diät, -en	diet
der Gastgeber, –	*host*
die Gastgeberin, -nen	
genauso	just as
herein·bitten, er hat hereingebeten	*to ask someone in, invite someone in*
die Lasagne, -n	*lasagne*
die Nachspeise, -n	dessert
nötig	necessary
die Nudel, -n	noodle
satt	full, sated
übrig: etw. übrig lassen, du lässt, er lässt, er hat übrig gelassen	remaining: to leave something over (resulting in leftovers)

Seite 35 — page 35

das Indefinitpronomen, –	*indefinite pronoun*

Seite 36 — page 36

aus·suchen	to select, pick out
der Berliner, –	*jelly doughnut*
das Ergebnis, -se	result
die Hefe (nur Singular)	*yeast*
der Klaben, –	*sweet loaf cake with dried fruit*
die Korinthe, -n	*currant*
der Kranz, ¨-e	*wreath*
der Lebkuchen, –	*German gingerbread*
das Leckerli, -s	*Swiss gingerbread with honey and nuts*
das Marzipan, -e	*marzipan*
das Mehl (nur Singular)	flour
das Nockerl, -n	*egg-based pastry popular in Salzburg*
das Orangeat (nur Singular)	*candied orange*
präsentieren	*to present*
die Printen (nur Plural)	*flat, spiced cookies associated with Aachen*
die Rosine, -n	*raisin*
der Stollen, –	*German Christmas bread with fruits*
die Torte, -n	tort, layer cake
das Zitronat (nur Singular)	*candied lemon*

Seite 37 — page 37

das Alpenland, ¨-er	*alpine country*
die Art, -en	type, variety
die Bankenstadt, ¨-e	*banking city*
beliebt	beloved
die Burg, -en	*fortress*
die Creme, -s	crème
das Gebäck (nur Singular)	baked goods
die Geburtsstadt, ¨-e	city of one's birth
die Großstadt, ¨-e	big city
die Heimat (nur Singular)	homeland, home country
je	ever
die Kalorie, -n	*calorie*
kcal	*abbreviation for calorie (counted in thousands)*
klingen, es hat geklungen	*to ring*
der Kontinent, -e	continent
die Marmeladenfüllung, -en	*marmelade filling*
das Mutterland, ¨-er	*motherland*
oberösterreichisch	*upper Austrian*
ostdeutsch	*east German*
die Sachertorte, -n	*Sacher tort*
die Süßigkeit, -en	*sweets*
die Süßspeise, -n	*sweet dish*
testen	*to test*
tja	*ehh... mmm...*
das Weihnachtsgebäck (nur Singular)	*Christmas baked goods*
wunderschön	*very beautiful*
zusammen·zählen	*to count together*

Arbeitsbuch	Workbook
Seite 105	**page 105**
streichen, er hat gestrichen	*to strike, cross out*
Seite 106	**page 106**
her·geben, du gibst her, er gibt her, er hat hergegeben	to hand over
hin·legen	to lay something down
das Laptop, -s	*laptop computer*
das Lotto (nur Singular)	*lottery*
der Sonnenschirm, -e	*parasol*
Seite 107	**page 107**
alkoholfrei	*non-alcoholic*
das Kännchen, –	*small coffee- or teapot (holds about 1.5 cups)*
der Käsekuchen, –	*cheesecake*
die Kirschtorte, -n	*cherry tort*
die Konditorei, -en	*pastry shop*
der Nusskuchen, –	*nutcake*
Seite 108	**page 108**
der Laut, -e	*sound*
Seite 109	**page 109**
die Bohne, -n	bean
die Lernkarte, -n	*study card*
die Rückseite, -n	*back/reverse side*
Seite 112	**page 112**
das Geschirr (nur Singular)	dishes

. /

ouns can be replaced by

iite pronoun, a noun
ınd if a noun is accompa-
ronoun.
ıe similar constructions
ı English, this becomes a
n always negates the
ıe."

ı	possessive pronoun
	Hier, das war ***deiner****.*
	Hier, das war ***deins****.*
	Hier, das war ***deine****.*
	Hier, das sind ***deine****.*

orresponding articles, but
he gender of the nouns

ord as their pronoun:
vord "some" would in

– *Hier, nimm* ***meinen****.* – Here, have **mine**.

When these pronouns serve as the complements of a verb that needs a direct object *(haben, nehmen, etc.),* the pronouns are accusative. Remember that the verb *haben* requires an accusative complement (direct object):

examples *Haben wir noch Nüsse?*
– ~~Ja, wir haben noch.~~
– Ja, wir haben noch ***welche.***

Do we still have nuts?
– Yes, we still have **some**.

	accusative	indefinite pronoun	negation	possessive pronoun
m	*Einen Apfel?*	*Ja, wir haben noch* ***einen.***	*Nein, wir haben* ***keinen*** *mehr.*	*Hier nimm* ***meinen.***
n	*Ein Croissant?*	*Ja, wir haben noch* ***eins.***	*Nein, wir haben* ***keins*** *mehr.*	*Hier, nimm* ***meins.***
f	*Eine Brezel?*	*Ja, wie haben noch* ***eine.***	*Nein, wir haben* ***keine*** *mehr.*	*Hier, nimm* ***meine.***
pl	*Nüsse?*	*Ja, wir haben noch* ***welche.***	*Nein, wir haben* ***keine*** *mehr.*	*Hier, nimm* ***meine.***

Just as in the case of articles, the only form in the accusative case that varies from the nominative is that of the masculine singular.

3 The particle *etwa*

examples *Ihr wollt doch nicht etwa eure Fahrräder mitnehmen, oder?*
Hast du etwa bis jetzt geschlafen?
Hast du etwa noch nicht gegessen?

You don't want to take your bikes with you, do you? (Don't tell me you're taking your bikes!)
You didn't get any sleep yet, did you?
Haven't you eaten yet? (Don't tell me you haven't eaten yet!)

The particle *etwa* in a closed question expresses that the speaker is posing a rhetorical question and is hoping for a contrary response. In English, this can take the form of a question or a "don't tell me" exclamation.

4 Adverbs in speech

examples

Die Küche *Da vorne*	*ist* *ist*	*da vorne.* *die Küche.*	
Wir *Morgen*	*haben* *haben*	*morgen* *wir*	*frei.* *frei.*
Der Bäcker hat *Vielleicht*	*hat* *hat*	*vielleicht* *der Bäcker*	*noch Nussschnecken.* *noch Nussschnecken.*
Wir *Meistens*	*trinken* *trinken*	*meistens* *wir*	*Orangensaft.* *Orangensaft.*
1	**2 (verb)**	**3**	

In Chapter 4 of *Schritte international 1,* we saw that adverbs are usually located in third position, after the subject and the conjugated verb. However, for purposes of emphasis, the adverb can also appear in the first position, trading places with the subject, so to speak.

5 Translate into English.

a *Das ist doch Guidos Computer, nicht?* ....?

– Nein, das ist meiner. Seiner steht da hinten. ....

b *Ich habe mein Buch vergessen.* ....

– Hier, du kannst meins nehmen. ....

c *Braucht ihr vielleicht einen Gameboy?* ....?

– Nein, danke. Unsere Kinder haben schon einen und einer ist genug! .... enough!

6 Translate into German.

a Would you give me a glass, please? ....?

– Sure, here's one. ....

b By the way, do we still have any bananas? ....?

– Yeah, there are still some. Do you want one? ....?

c Would you like a coffee? ....?

– No thanks, I don't want any. ....

d I can't find my pen. Can I use yours? ....?

– Yes, sure. ....

7 Translate into German.

a Most of the time, I have granola for breakfast. ....

– Don't you drink any coffee? ....?

– No, almost never. ....

b Maybe we should review a little. ....

Tomorrow I want to take a test. ....

– What a shame! Can't we play a game instead? (That is what I would rather do.) .... lieber ....?

c Surely you're tired. The trip was long. ....:

I'll take you to a hotel. ....:

– No, thanks very much. I slept on the ....

train. ....:

Listening and Pronunciation

Pronunciation of <s>

Pause • *Straße*
Gläser • *Messer*

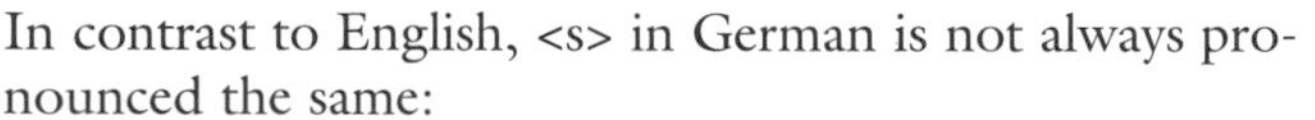

In contrast to English, <s> in German is not always pronounced the same:
At the beginning of a word or syllable, before a vowel or between two vowels, it has the sound of the voiced, English <z>, (*Pau-se*, *Sa-lat*).
However, when it appears at the end of a word or syllable, or when it is doubled or appears as a ß (*Eis*, *Messer*, *Straße*), it sounds like the voiceless English <s>.
Still, there are German-speaking areas, particularly the more southerly ones (in Bavaria or Austria, for example) where there is no difference in the initial s and the final or doubled s; they are all voiceless like the English <s>.

Pronunciation of <y>

Berufstyp • *Ägypten*

In German, <y> is prounced the same as <ü> (*Tür*).

Familiarity and Understanding

It's not easy being green

In Austria, Switzerland and Germany, interest in environmental issues, health and clean living is high, though figures on consumption of organic products are not exactly spectacular: only 3% of foods consumed are organic, but that 5% represents a 15% increase in 2008 over the previous year. In years where there have been environmental scandals or disasters, organic consumption has increased up to 35%.

Among factors contributing to this awareness are population density and relative affluence, but the origins of organic agriculture reach back to the 1920s, when one trend known as anthroposophy, founded by Rudolf Steiner, sought to harmonize humanity with nature and the cosmos.

Organic agriculture is divided into various "schools" according to the degree of ecological control; for example, whether fertilizers of animal origin are used, whether feed is grown on site or brought in, or whether it has been mixed with non-biological products. The majority of producers have joined together in various associations such as *Bioland*, *Demeter* (an organization with anthroposophic origins), *Gäa e.V.*, most prevalent in the eastern states of Germany, or *Bio Suisse* and *Bio Austria* respectively. Many farms sell their products directly to consumers as well as to supermarkets carrying products free of chemical or genetic alterations or irradiation. So-called *Reformhäuser*, a sort of health food store, specialize in such products.

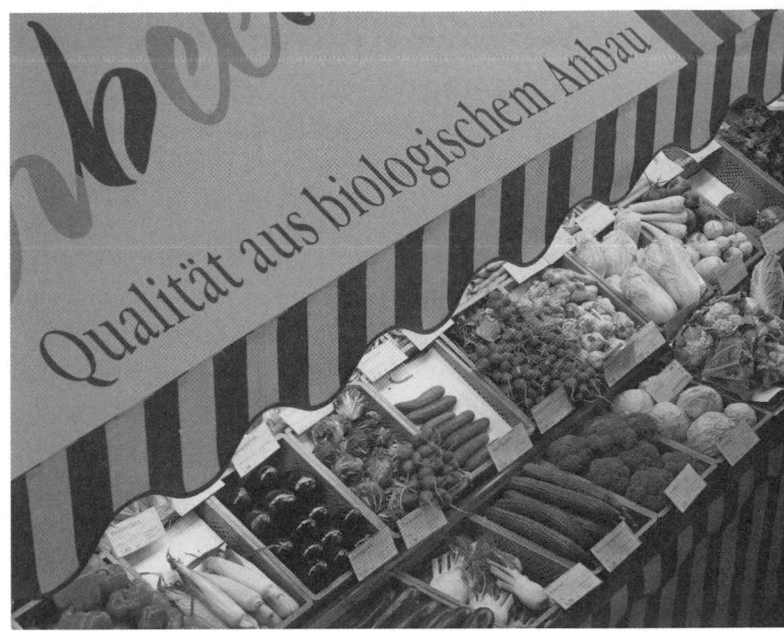

Yellow: the new green?

On a trip through northern Germany in the spring, it can appear that when the sun shines, the rapeseed fields are ablaze, as the Romanian-German poet Herta Müller wrote. Northern Germany can seem to be covered with thousands and thousands of fields of this cruciferous plant whose flower boasts an intense yellow hue. The rapeseed is experiencing a boom in "traditional" German agriculture, as this aesthetically appealing plant, already prized as far back as the Middle Ages for its high oil content (it was used as a light source before the discovery of petroleum) is now being processed into biodiesel fuel. Production in this industry is expected to create more independence from petroleum by replacing large quantities of gasoline. However, many experts warn about carbon dioxide emissions from processing (nitrous oxide is another greenhouse gas byproduct of biodiesel production from rapeseed) and soil erosion due to monoculture. In addition, these "energy" fields displace relatively profitable foodstuff farming, since biodiesel farming requires a lot more ground than traditional agriculture. Furthermore, the amount of energy spent harvesting rapeseed is comparable to the energy yield from the crop. Hence, many choose to refer to biodiesel from rapeseed as *Agrodiesel*, since it does not appear to fulfill as much promise as many would hope.

But this does not prevent these yellow fields in spring from casting their spell on passers-by ...

Two Inventive, Entreprenurial Women / Coffee without grounds

Though nowadays in the German-speaking countries, it is more fashionable to drink Italian-style espresso coffee, traditional coffee in Germany is brewed by passing boiling water through a paper filter holding the ground beans. The paper filter was the idea of Dresden housewife Melitta Bentz, who received the patent for her invention in 1908. Originally wishing to avoid the grounds at the end of a cup of coffee, she tore a page from her son's notebook, fashioned it into a funnel and the rest was history.

Shortly thereafter, Melitta and her family realized the potential of her idea, and after obtaining the patent and entering it into the merchant registry, they entered into manufacturing the filters, holders and coffeepots. 10 years on, Melitta had about 100 employees working shifts in the factory. Currently, the business has over 3,500 workers.

The *Currywurst* and its inventor

Herta Heuwer was the proprietress of a wurst stand during the 1950s in Berlin. She sold sausages with a sauce made from a tomato base, Indian spices such as curry, Worcestershire sauce and other ingredients. People took to her sauce like they had to Coca-Cola. Herta Heuwer then had an idea: if Coca-Cola could do it, so could she, and she decided to patent her recipe. After receiving her patent, Herta Heuwer built a larger *Imbiss* (fast food stand) in Berlin with 19 women working there all day.

Sampling a *Currywurst* is part of the Berlin tourist experience, though clearly not for vegetarians. If one believes the marketing, then *Currywurst* is Germany's most famous food, counting former Chancellor Gerhard Schröder among its greatest supporters. In memory of Herta Heuwer, the city of Berlin erected a marker at the intersection of *Kantstraße* and *Kaiser-Friedrich-Straße*, in the center of the capital, where she had her business. Herta Heuwer died in 1999, but the *Currywurst* continues to hold so much significance that, in 2007, a museum devoted to the *Currywurst* was erected that will hopefully attract 350,000 visitors annually.

How one sausage equals an equator

In southern Germany and especially in Bavaria, they say, it's not a good idea to order a *Currywurst*, as their specialty is the *Weißwurst*, a white sausage boiled in water and traditionally served with sweet mustard. It is made with beef and pork finely ground and then seasoned, and stuffed into a rather tough skin. It is recommended that those unaccustomed to such sausage casings simply split the skin and remove it before eating the meat. Tradition says that *Weißwurst* should be eaten no later than noon, but this tradition is more grounded in an era of limited refrigeration; *Weißwurst* is now eaten at any time.

Northern and southern Germany are separated by a border, known humorously as the *Weißwurstäquator (Weißwurst* equator*)*, an ancient line separating the Kingdom of Bavaria from the rest of Germany. The border varies however – sometimes it's the Danube, sometimes the Main river – but wherever it lies, it is the demarcation line between north and south.

The same thing occurs in Switzerland, where the German-speaking part meets the Francophone section along the *Röstigraben* (the *Rösti* trench, referencing a grated potato dish that is a specialty of the German-speaking area of the country).

Historical Fragments

From the French Revolution to Restoration (1789–1815)

The French Revolution, the confusion surrounding the founding of the First Republic, and the execution of King Louis XVI in 1793 led to a number of wars between European monarchies.

In 1792, France declared war on the Holy Roman Empire. Prussia agreed to certain peace terms, having already annexed parts of Poland where troops were needed. The Holy Roman Empire (its full name was actually "Holy Roman Empire of the German Nation") lost Alsace and Lorraine, which became French territories. When Napoleon took charge of the war and advanced on the nations in northern and eastern Europe, he took the opportunity to reorganize numerous things: the Church lost all its assets, and those states who had agreed with Napoleon, such as Baden or Bavaria, among others, significantly increased their territories. In 1806, some of those states officially declared themselves allies of Napoleon and formed their own Alliance, the *Rheinbund* or Rhine Federation. This meant the end of the Holy Roman Empire under Habsburg rule.
Prussia protested but eventually lost the struggle, along with two-thirds of its territory.
For his part, Napoleon was immersed in wars against Spain and Portugal but he was also at the apex of his power: all German states were dependent upon him, had to pay taxes and provide him with troops. Russia put an end to his victories in 1812–1813, and with the defeat of his army, began the wars of liberation. The eastern Germany city of Leipzig was the scene of a bloody battle, the *Völkerschlacht* (Battle of Nations) when in four days, from the 16th to the 19th of October 1813, about 100,000 died or were seriously injured. This signaled the end of the Napoleonic system; Napoleon abdicated, was exiled to the island of Elba, and later, after another initially victorious attempt, but culminating in the fracas at Waterloo, was finally banished to the remote Atlantic island of Saint Helena.

The French Revolution had unforeseeable consequences, and not only for Germany, whose entire political and state landscape was completely changed. Whereas prior to the 1789 French Revolution it had existed as numerous small states, Napoleon created a conglomeration of more than 300 states which later, at the Congress of Vienna in 1815, would be consolidated down to 39.

The revolution led to reforms in the German states in the areas of government and education policy as well as the economy and the army. German nationalism, ignited by the French Revolution, had as its goal the unification of the German states, though not without sowing seeds of destructive forces.

And so German Question was born, and no one could have guessed that it would not be resolved until 1990, when the German borders were finally recognized by the major powers, its neighbor states and the German people.

Self-Evaluation

Bon Appetit!

When listening, I can understand (Hören)

- Information on social customs such as an invitation
- Conversations on distinct situations in a restaurant
- Short songs on culinary topics: i.e., *„Currywurst“*

In written texts, I can understand (Lesen)

- Informative pamphlets: *„Sind Sie oft erkältet? Stärken Sie Ihr Immunsystem …“*
- Short texts on social customs: *„Küsse auf die Wange sind ein noch neuer Trend …“*
- Recipes for regional specialties and desserts, and short texts on their origins
- A bar or restaurant menu
- Short magazine texts on food

I can produce the following oral structures (Sprechen)

- Talk about breakfast and other gastronomical customs
- Look for a place to sit: *„Entschuldigung, ist hier noch frei?“*
- Make requests, pay, and complain in a restaurant: *„Ich nehme die Kürbiscremesuppe …“*
- Make small talk at a table: *„Setzt euch doch. Was möchtet ihr trinken?“*
- Say what I like to eat and drink: *„Ich esse gerne scharf.“*
- Express the frequency of what I do: *„Meistens trinke ich Kaffee zum Frühstück.“*

I can produce the following written texts (Schreiben)

- Accepting or declining an invitation in writing: *„Liebe Michaela, vielen Dank für deine Einladung. Es tut mir sehr leid …“*
- Description of a person's habits: *„Er/sie geht oft spazieren, er geht manchmal in die Disco, …“*
- An e-mail describing a meal to which I was invited

Kursbuch	Textbook

Seite 38 — page 38

Seite 38	page 38
die Arbeitswelt (nur Singular)	*world of work*
der Handwerker, –	craftsman specializing in hand work
das Produkt, -e	product
der Schreiner, –	*carpenter, woodworker*
der Teig, -e	*dough*

Seite 39 — page 39

Seite 39	page 39
aus·geben, du gibst aus, er gibt aus, er hat ausgegeben	to spend (money)
nachts	nights
sparen	to save (money or time)

Seite 40 — page 40

Seite 40	page 40
arrogant	*arrogant*
beachten	to observe, be mindful of
beenden	*to end*
der Berufsanfänger, –	*a beginner in a given profession*
der Gewinner, –	*winner*
merken (sich)	to note (mentally), memorize
sachlich	*objective, neutral*
so ... wie	as ... as
die Starthilfe, -n	*help getting started*
die Überstunde, -n	overtime
übertreiben, er hat übertrieben	*to exaggerate*
zu·gehen, er ist zugegangen	*to approach, go up to*

Seite 41 — page 41

Seite 41	page 41
ab·schließen, er hat abgeschlossen	to close, lock
an·geben, du gibst an, er gibt an, er hat angegeben	*to indicate*
aus·schalten	to turn/switch off
betrunken	drunk, inebriated
der Empfang, ¨-e	reception
die Kantine, -n	cantina, cafeteria
die Lust (nur Singular)	desire, interest
das Material, Materialien	material
nachmittags	afternoons
der Praktikumsplatz, ¨-e	*internship position*
die Quittung, -en	receipt
spülen	to rinse, wash (dishes)
die Stellenanzeige, -n	classified job ad
stören	to disturb, disrupt
stundenweise	*by the hour*
Taxi fahren, du fährst, er fährt, er ist Taxi gefahren	to drive a taxi
die Teilzeit (nur Singular)	*part time (as in employment)*
übersetzen	to translate
zusammen·setzen	*to put together, combine*

Seite 42 — page 42

Seite 42	page 42
die Abteilung, -en	department
der Arbeitsplatz, ¨-e	workplace, job
aus·richten	*to report, give word*
außer: außer Haus	outside: away from the office
die Durchwahl, -en	*extension, direct line*
die Exportabteilung, -en	*export department*
die Export-Importabteilung, -en	*import-export department*
gleichfalls	same to you; likewise

Seite 43 — page 43

Seite 43	page 43
Ahnung: keine Ahnung	*idea, inkling: no idea*
der/die Angestellte, -n	white-collar employee, office employee
der Arbeitnehmer, –	employee
betreffen	*to relate to, be in regard to*
der Durchschnitt (nur Singular)	*average*
durchschnittlich	on average
folgen	to follow
der Freizeitweltmeister, –	*world champion of free time*
insgesamt	in total, all together
das Institut, -e	institute
Japan	*Japan*
Luxemburg	Luxemburg
die Spitze, -n	*point, summit*
die Studie, -n	*study, research project*
der Tag der Deutschen Einheit (nur Singular)	Day of German Unity (German national holiday)
untere	lower
der Urlaubstag, -e	*vacation day*
weg·fahren, du fährst weg, er fährt weg, er ist weggefahren	to drive off or drive away
zumindest	*at least*
zweimal	twice

Seite 44 — page 44

Seite 44	page 44
der Adler, –	*eagle*
ähnlich	similar
die Auflösung, -en	*here: key*
die Begabung, -en	*gift, talent*
der Berufstest, -s	*occupational aptitude test*
der Berufstyp, -en	*type of occupation*
die Bohrmaschine, -n	*boring/drilling machine*
eindeutig	*clearly, explicitly*
erkennen, er hat erkannt	to recognize
der Exportartikel, –	*export article*
der Hammer, ¨-e	hammer
der Handelspartner, –	*trading partner*
das Holz, ¨-er	wood
die Krankenschwester, -n	nurse
leicht	easy, light
der Meister, –	master
der Nagel, ¨-e	nail
das Nest, -er	nest
Öko	*eco-*
sozial	social
das Symbol, -e	symbol
der Typ, -en	guy

der Vogel, ¨	bird
der Wald, ¨er	*forest*
die Zusammenarbeit (nur Singular)	cooperation, working together

Seite 45	page 45
der Nebensatz, ¨e	*subordinate clause*

Seite 46	page 46
die Armee, -n	*army*
der Astronaut, -en	*astronaut*
darauf	on it
die Design-Abteilung, -en	*design department*
der Dosenöffner, –	*can opener*
die Expedition, -en	*expedition*
der Extrembergsteiger, –	*extreme mountain climber*
die Funktion, -en	*function*
der Gebrauch (nur Singular)	*use*
genial	*brilliant, genius-like*
gründen	to found, establish
häufig	common, often
irgendwo	somewhere
kaputtgehen, es ist kaputtgegangen	to break, "go kerplooey"
der Korkenzieher, –	*corkscrew*
der Kunststoff, -e	artificial material
der Messerschmied, -e	*knife maker, cutler*
das Offiziersmesser, –	*Swiss Army knife (issued to officers)*
das Soldatenmesser, –	*Swiss Army knife (issued to troops)*
das Taschenmesser, –	*pocket knife*
überleben	*to survive*
die Weltraum (nur Singular)	*outer space*
weltweit	*world-wide*

Seite 47	page 47
der Arbeitgeber, –	employer
der Export, -e	export
das Familienunternehmen, –	*family business*
der Firmengründer, –	*company founder*
industriell	*industrial*
jetzige	*current, at this time*
die Kündigung, -en	giving notice, firing
der Mitarbeiter, –	coworker
das Prozent, -e	percent
der Urenkel, –	*great-grandchild*
wirtschaftlich	*economic*

Arbeitsbuch — Workbook

Seite 116	page 116
das Büromaterial, -materialien	*office material*

Seite 119	page 119
aus·tragen, du trägst aus, er trägt aus, er hat ausgetragen	*to carry out*
aus·üben	*to exercise, carry out*
betreuen	to tend to, take care of
die Fahrt, -en	trip
die Gaststätte, -n	inn
gelten, es gilt, es hat gegolten	to be valid as
das Gesetz, -e	law
die Nachhilfe (nur Singular)	*tutoring*
die Schulferien (nur Plural)	*school break*
die Tätigkeit, -en	activity

1 Suggestions: the verb *sollen* in subjunctive II *(Ratschlag: sollen im Konjunktiv II)*

examples		
	Sie sollten jetzt (mal) nach Hause gehen.	You really should go home now.
	Du solltest vielleicht doch etwas anderes anziehen.	Perhaps you should put something else on.

In Chapter 9 of *Schritte international 2* we looked at how, when suggesting or recommending something, you can use the imperative *(Gehen Sie doch mal zur Touristeninformation!)*, or the modal verb *müssen (Wir müssen unbedingt mal in den Dom gehen.)*.
Another possibility when making a suggestion or recommendation is the modal verb *sollen*, in the form of *Konjunktiv II*. In such statements, the particles *mal*, *doch* or *unbedingt* often appear *(Den solltest du mal besuchen. / Sie sollten unbedingt zum Arzt gehen.)*. In general, a recommendation using *sollt-* has a gentler, less imperious effect than an imperative or a suggestion with *müssen*.

You can now see that the modal verb *„möchten"* does not have an infinitive form *„möchten"* but is really the *Konjunktiv II* of the verb *mögen* (*Schritte international 1*, Chapter 6).

Compare:

sollen	*„möchten"*
ich sollte	*ich möchte*
du solltest	*du möchtest*
er/sie sollte	*er/sie möchte*
wir sollten	*wir möchten*
ihr solltet	*ihr möchtet*
sie/Sie sollten	*sie/Sie möchten*

2 The conjunction *wenn (Konjunktion wenn)*

a Main clause before a subordinate (dependent) clause *(Hauptsatz vor dem Nebensatz)*

examples		
	*Fragen Sie mich bitte, **wenn** Sie etwas brauchen.*	Please ask me if you need something.
	*Susanne will nur stundenweise arbeiten, **wenn** das Baby da ist.*	Susanne only wants to work on an hourly basis when the baby arrives.

The conjunction *wenn* has two functions: it can express both a temporal relationship (when) as well as a conditional one (if). As you can see in the examples above, *wenn* introduces a subordinate, or dependent clause: the conjugated verb is in final position and the subordinate clause is set off from the main clause by a comma (see Chapter 1, The conjunction *weil*).

b Subordinate clause before the main clause *(Nebensatz vor dem Hauptsatz)*

examples		
	***Wenn** Sie etwas brauchen, (dann) fragen Sie mich bitte.*	If you need something, (then) ask me.
	***Wenn** das Baby da ist, (dann) will Susanne nur stundenweise arbeiten.*	When the baby is there, Susanne only wants to work on an hourly basis.

A subordinate clause with *wenn* can come before or after the main clause. If the subordinate clause with *wenn* comes first in the sentence, then the entire clause functions as the first element of the sentence and the conjugated verb in the main clause comes immediately after the comma separating the clauses, with the subject following the verb.
The main clause may also begin with the adverb *dann* (then), but just like in English, this is not required. Using *dann* does not change the verb-subject word order.

3 The indefinite pronouns *jemand, niemand, etwas, nichts*

examples

*Ist denn **jemand** aus der Abteilung da?*	Is anyone from the department there?
*Nein, da ist im Moment **niemand** da.*	No, at the moment no one is there.
*Hat **jemand** angerufen?*	Did someone/anyone call?
*Ja, aber ich habe **seinen** Namen vergessen.*	Yes, but I forgot (their) his name.
*Kann ich **etwas** ausrichten?*	Can I pass something on?
Nein danke, ich rufe nochmal an.	No, thanks, I'll call again.
*Hast du **etwas** verstanden?*	Did you understand anything?
*Nein, ich habe **nichts** verstanden.*	No, I didn't understand a thing (I understood nothing).

The indefinite pronoun *jemand* refers only to people. Its corresponding possessive article is *sein* (like *man, jemand* is gender neutral, but defaults to the masculine forms of possessives. In English, we avoid the problem of gender agreement in speech by using the plural "their", but in German, this is not the case.) The negative form of *jemand* is *niemand.*
The indefinite pronoun *etwas* and its negative counterpart *nichts* refer to things or circumstances and never to people.
The indefinite pronoun *nichts* does not correspond to the negation *nicht* in any way:
- The pronoun *nichts* replaces nouns for which there is a zero quantity:
  Ich hatte kein Geld, keinen Pass, kein Flugticket, ich hatte nichts mehr.
- The negation *nicht* makes nouns, verbs or adjectives negative:
  Ich habe die Frage nicht verstanden.
  Herr Kraus ist gerade nicht am Platz.
  Ich lese nicht, ich höre Musik.
  Die Wohnung ist nicht teuer.

4 Translate into English.

a *Hm! Das Eis ist aber lecker! Das* ....
solltest du mal probieren! ....!
– Nein danke, ich esse lieber Obst. ....

b *Ihr solltet nicht so lange duschen,* ....
Wasser ist teuer. ....
– Ich war doch nur 5 Minuten unter ....
der Dusche! ....!

c *Tom ist heute Morgen schon wieder* ....
zu spät gekommen. ....
– Wir sollten vielleicht mal mit ihm sprechen. ....

d *Was möchtest du denn essen? Such dir* ....
etwas aus! ....!
– Nein, danke, ich möchte jetzt nichts essen. ....

e *Hat jemand seine Autoschlüssel verloren? Der Hausmeister hat welche gefunden.*
– Nein, in unserer Gruppe kommt niemand mit dem Auto.

5 Translate into German.

a What should we do when we're done with the exercise?
– You can review the vocabulary from Chapter 3.

b If Mr. Miller calls, please make an appointment with him for Friday at 12.
– On Friday at 12 you have to go to the doctor!

c What happened? Why aren't you coming?
– I had a problem with the car. If I'm not there at 10, please start (anyway). *schon*

6 Translate into German.

a Has anyone seen my purse?
– Yes, you set it on the chair.
– It's terrible, I'm always looking for something!

b Is anyone from the German department here?
– Sorry, at the moment, no one is there. Should I pass something on?

c Can you connect me to Ms. Weber, please?
– Sorry, Ms. Weber isn't in the office today. Should she call you back?
– No thanks, I'll call again tomorrow. *noch einmal*

Listening and Pronunciation

Pronunciation of <ch>

ich ● *auch*
dich ● *doch*
Gespräch ● *Sprache*
Kirche
Brötchen

Two different sounds in German correspond to the written <ch>, one which sounds like *ich* and the other which sounds like *ach*. The first one, known in German as *ich-Laut*, follows the vowels <e, i, ä, ö, ü, ei, äu>; and the second one, known as *ach-Laut*, follows < a, o, u, au>.
In the first group, the vowels in question are higher up in the mouth, and as such the sound of the <ch> is closer to that of a cat's hiss, while the second group of vowels sit lower in the mouth, leaving the <ch> closer to the throat. The second one, then, the *ach-Laut*, is similar to the Scottish <ch>. While it borders on being guttural, however, it is not in the throat. It does not sound like the speaker is coughing up something.

Stress of sentence elements

Guten <u>Morgen</u>. Es hat jemand für dich <u>angerufen</u>.

As in English, new or more relevant information in a sentence is stressed. In neutral statements, new or more relevant information tends to go to the end of a German sentence, and as such, it has the primary stress in the overall sentence. Note that in the case of past participles with separable prefixes, that prefix will carry the main stress.

Familiarity and Understanding

Keeping Germany competitive

1 of every 3 German Euros comes from exports, and Germany is largely dependent on foreign trade. Germany is the largest exporter on earth, ahead of the U.S., Japan and even China. This means that every fourth job in Germany is dependent upon the chain of consumption abroad and the "Made in Germany" image that products have around the world. In the face of globalization, making cheaper production in other countries ever easier, this image is of crucial importance.

The country to which Germany exports most is France, and Europe as a whole absorbs 74.4% of products produced in Germany. Exports to the Americas total 11.5% while 11.3% go to Asia and Africa receives 1.9%.

The most exported product remains the automobile, and among the top five German exporters, the top two are auto manufacturers: Daimler sits in first place, followed by Volkswagen. Fifth place is also held by an auto manufacturer, BMW. In third place is Siemens, and in fourth place the energy company e.on.

Machinery is the number two export from Germany, followed by chemicals. However, goods are increasingly prefabricated elsewhere, indicating that major investment is slowly leaving the country, threatening jobs in Germany.

Indexes such as the World Economic Forum's Global Competitiveness Index place Germany relatively highly in 7th place out of 134 nations for 2008–09, but they are not so optimistic when looking at factors relating to future economic health, such as innovation, education, and numerous factors relative to labor market efficiency, where Germany ranks much lower. What causes such a gap? Studies say that Germany is home to a productive sector internationally, but the competitive domestic market is relatively cautious and burdened by various beaurocratic demands.

Change is needed, and studies suggest macroeconomic reforms to major social and economic structures are key. But what might these reforms be? Greater labor flexibility, for starters, followed by lower labor costs and a more rigorous educational system, are just a few of the hurdles that must be overcome. Compared to Switzerland, for example, Germany still has a relatively high unemployment rate.

And, speaking of Switzerland, this neighboring country counts foreigners as 20% of its resident population. In recent years, the largest group entering Switzerland has been Germans, comprising 56% of all foreign residents, especially in the service sector, hotels and restaurants. But Switzerland is also highly attractive to many German scientists who enjoy less bureaucracy and more freedom for their research. They also appreciate that Swiss companies spend more money on R & D than their German neighbors, that protection of intellectual property is strong and that Swiss institutions have a reputation for providing good service to the citizenry. With these positive attributes, Switzerland earned second place in the Global Competitiveness Index – surpassed only by the United States.

Hergestellt in Japan? No: Made in Germany!

One day, one of the inventors of the MP3 flew to Japan to visit a showroom. In Tokyo, he took the subway and sat next to a young man with MP3 earbuds on. The scientist became interested in the latest generation model and the two began to talk. Proudly, the young man told the foreigner it was a Japanese invention.
The inventor smiled, but remained silent ... His nationality? German.

Millions of people own one, but few know that the MP3 codec was actually a German invention dating back to the early 1990s. It was developed at the Fraunhofer Institute in Erlangen, near Nuremberg. The idea of transmitting data and voice at very high quality via phone lines was born back in the 1970s. In the following years and decades, scientists were able to first encode audio data and then compress it: the first portable MP3 player only had a four song capacity. Today, in Germany alone, MP3 technology provides jobs to more than 10,000 people, and its turnover, calculated at 1.5 billion Euros (between sales of players, music, and data that can be downloaded via the Internet), is not insignificant, either. The Fraunhofer Institute has also made good money thanks to MP3; in 2006 alone, license fees brought in about $85 million. This scientific institute, devoted to applied science and research, is designed to serve society and private industry by serving as a bridge between research and application. It is partly a public institution and partially private; 40% of the financing for the *Fraunhofer-Gesellschaft* (Fraunhofer Society) comes from state and federal governments, but the rest is privately financed. There are 56 Fraunhofer Institutes in Germany with 12,400 employees and researchers. Their research spans about 80 different fields, including information technology, biomedical technology, molecular biology, research materials (including wood), nanotechnology, solar energy, software, packaging materials, traffic systems and infrastructure. The Society and the Institutes were named for Joseph Fraunhofer, an astronomer, physicist, optician and inventor in the early 19th century.

A 600,000,000-piece jigsaw puzzle

Imagine trying to assemble a jigsaw puzzle with 600,000,000 pieces: yes, six hundred million pieces, stored in 16,250 bags. Each piece came originally from a sheet of paper that was broken down to anywhere from 8 to 30 pieces. The challenge now is to put these pieces back into order. To give a little perspective on the scope of such a task, one person would need 24,000 years, while 30 people could do in about 800 years. But why do this at all?

In the fall of 1989, the GDR collapsed and the wall between West and East Germany opened. Just prior to the Wall's fall and in the months of uncertainty that ensued, the *Stasi* (abbreviation for *Ministerium für Staatssicherheit*, the GDR secret police) tried to destroy as much of the surveillance documentation they had amassed on GDR citizens, and they worked as fast as they could. When mechanical shredders could not keep up, they started tearing papers by hand. This went on until January of 1990, until mass demonstrations spilled into the *Stasi* headquarters and halted the destruction. After 40 years of being spied on, informed upon and intimidated (the Oscar-winning film *"Das Leben der Anderen"* gives a very accurate depiction of what transpired during those years), people wanted to know what the *Stasi* had on them.

By October of 2000, approximately 1.7 million people had asked to see their files. These individuals were not only citizens of the former GDR, but also of other nations. Even though the *Stasi* had managed to destroy only 5% of their surveillance files, that still amounted to about 45 million documents torn into about 600 million pieces. Once again, enter Fraunhofer: the Fraunhofer Institute for Production Systems and Design Technology, working together with the Stasi Records Office, developed a digital scanning project which digitally recreates the documents by matching edges, text and other markers on both sides of each piece of paper. 400 of the 16,000 bags of document remains are currently stored on 22 terabytes of memory in a pilot project which, if successful, will then lead to a restoration project involving hundreds of computers aiding specialists to reconstruct and analyze the documents over at least a decade. The cost of the entire project is currently estimated at about $30 million, but with 5000 to 6000 people requesting access to their files each month, demand is obviously in significant supply.

The Max Planck Institute

As you have read above, the *Fraunhofer-Gesellschaft* is an extremely large network of scientific and technical institutes dedicated to applied research which bridges the gap between academics and industy. The *Max-Planck-Gesellschaft,* in contrast, is devoted to pure research: in the fields of biology, medicine, chemistry, physics on the one hand, and on the other, in the humanities and social sciences. With 17 winners since 1948, the *Max-Planck-Gesellschaft*, named for the quantum mechanical physicist Max Planck (1858–1947), is the record-holder for independent institutions producing Nobel laureates. The 80 individual Institutes work in close cooperation with universities, though they are independent of all other institutions. They are home to about 4200 scientists doing research and around 9000 guest researchers at any given time. After AT&T and the Argonne National Laboratory in the United States, the Max-Planck-Gesellschaft is the largest research institution in the world.

Historical Fragments

The Decade of Classicism

The fact that Germany was divided into hundreds of sovereign states did not favor the development of a German cultural tradition. Artists were dependent upon and subject to the ruling aristocracy of their particular location, and there was no bourgeoisie like that which existed in France or Great Britain, and hence no open market for works of art.

Vienna's imperial court became the center of the musical universe in the 18th century. Haydn and Mozart lived there, where Mozart was first Haydn's pupil and later colleague. Beethoven was also a pupil of Haydn. During the last decade of the 18th century, their works led to what is now known as Vienna Classicism (*Wiener Klassik).*

At the same time, in the same decade, a small group of writers formed the core of the Classical era in German literature, based in Weimar, the capital of a small German prinicipality. Here, Duchess Anna Amalia brought together the elite of German writers in Weimar: Goethe, Schiller, Herder, Hölderlin and Jean Paul, among others, creating what came to be known as Weimar Classicism (*Weimarer Klassik*). Goethe and Schiller were the foremost figures of this period, and their correspondence served as the manifesto *per se* of German classical literature and art. For Herder, language was the most profound expression of a nation and its character. Several authors discovered folk culture, songs, poems and stories as links within their divided nation. The authors of classical Weimar focused on Greek and Roman antiquity, its expression of beauty, and its image of man.

On the heels of the French Revolution and under the influence of philosopher Immanuel Kant (1724–1804), human dignity was considered binding on the fundamentals of human rights. It should come as no surprise that Paris became a focal point for many figures in the period, with its early promise of democracy and freedom of expression. But the Revolution's excesses, especially Louis XVI's execution in 1793, then soured their enthusiasm.

Napoleon arrived and initiated a war against the German states. What at the start of the French Revolution had been enthusiasm for its ideals became pure nationalism in opposition to Napoleon, and the war against him clearly had a unifying effect, demonstrated in the attempts to unite Germany as a nation of free men in the decades that followed. Still, another 100 years would pass before these ideals were realized.

The city of Weimar returned to prominence in 1919 with the establishment of the Weimar Republic after World War I. The location was deliberately chosen to connect with the idea of a cultural nation as a member of an international community of nations, and hence its name: the Weimar Republic.

It lasted until 1933 when Hitler came to power, repealed the Weimar constitution and jailed his opponents. In 1937, the construction of the concentration camp of Buchenwald, near Weimar, completely compromised the memory of the ideals of Weimar Classicism.

Self-Evaluation

The World of Work

When listening, I can understand (Hören)

- An interview about a particular job: *„Sie backen ja sicher ein sehr gutes Brot, oder?“*
- Descriptive statements about different jobs and the tasks involved in them
- Phone conversations at work
- Short messages on an answering machine

In written texts, I can understand (Lesen)

- Simple magazine texts: *„Die ersten 100 Tage im Beruf. Was Sie beachten sollten …“*
- Concise descriptions: *Workshop Bewerbung: Wie formuliert man das Bewerbungsschreiben?*
- A brief test to identify which job is best for me
- Specific information on manufactured goods: *Taschenmesser*

I can produce the following oral structures (Sprechen)

- Offer others advice: *„Vielleicht sollten Sie doch etwas anderes anziehen!“*
- Express conditions: *„Wenn du keine Lust mehr auf deinen Job hast, …“*
- Call a business by phone, leave a voice mail message and ask to speak with someone: *„Guten Tag, hier ist … Könnten Sie mich bitte …“*
- Talk about vacations and holiday celebrations
- Talk about my feelings and opinions regarding my profession

I can produce the following written texts (Schreiben)

- E-mail messages on notices, arranged appointments, and suggested activities: *„Lieber Herr Bauer, Frau Breiter hat angerufen …“*

Kursbuch	Textbook

Seite 48 — page 48

Seite 48	page 48
bügeln	*to iron*
dünn	thin
die Fitness (nur Singular)	*fitness*
die Gymnastik (nur Singular)	exercise
konzentrieren (sich)	to concentrate
woran	about what

Seite 49 — page 49

Seite 49	page 49
ach was	oh, come on; you must be kidding
bewegen (sich)	to move
das Freibad, ¨er	*outdoor swimming pool*
das Hallenbad, ¨er	*indoor swimming pool*
die Mathematik (Mathe) (nur Singular)	mathematics (math; maths)
nachher	afterwards
regelmäßig	regularly, at regular intervals
der Spiegel, –	mirror
die Sportart, -en	*type of sport*
völlig	completely, fully

Seite 50 — page 50

Seite 50	page 50
ärgern (sich)	to aggravate, to be aggravated
aus·ruhen (sich)	to calm (oneself) down
aus·ziehen (sich), er hat (sich) ausgezogen	to get undressed, disrobe
d.h.	*in other words; i.e.*
erkältet	ill with a cold
ernähren (sich)	to nourish (oneself)
das Gesundheitsplakat, -e	*health poster*
der Gesundheitstipp, -s	*health tip*
hoch·legen	*to put up, rest elevated*
das Immunsystem, -e	*immune system*
die Konzentrationsübung, -en	*concentration exercise*
der Lärm (nur Singular)	noise
reflexiv: reflexives Verb	*reflexive: reflexive verb*
runter·fallen, du fällst runter, er fällt runter, er ist runtergefallen	*to fall down (from a higher point to a lower one)*
schwach	weak
stärken	*to strengthen*

Seite 51 — page 51

Seite 51	page 51
beschweren (sich)	to complain
die Bewegung, -en	movement
das Fußballergebnis, -se	*football result (final score)*
kaum	hardly
die Kleinigkeit, -en	*small thing or matter*
die Modezeitschrift, -en	*fashion magazine*
der Professor, -en	professor
die Sportnachrichten (nur Plural)	*sports news*
die Wettervorhersage, -n	*weather forecast*

Seite 52 — page 52

Seite 52	page 52
der Braten, –	roast
brutal	*brutal*
daran	*here:* it
das Eishockey (nur Singular)	*ice hockey*
die Eishockey-Saison, -s	*ice hockey season*
erinnern (sich)	to remind (remember)
das Foul, -s	*foul*
das Frauenhandball (nur Singular)	*women's handball*
die Goldmedaille, -n	*gold medal*
das Handball (nur Singular)	*handball*
los·gehen, es ist losgegangen	to get going, start up
die Olympiade, -n	*Olympics*
der Quatsch (nur Singular)	nonsense, malarkey, bunk, bull
der Sonntagmittag, -e	Sunday noon
wofür	for what?
worauf	*here:* to what, for what

Seite 53 — page 53

Seite 53	page 53
der Anfänger, –	*beginner*
die Busfahrt, -en	bus trip
die Einzelstunde, -n	*individual hour (of instruction)*
empfehlen, du empfiehlst, er empfiehlt, er hat empfohlen	to recommend
der/die Fortgeschrittene, -n	*advanced (pupil, student)*
gern geschehen	my pleasure, don't mention it
das Golf (nur Singular)	*golf*
das Golfhotel, -s	*golf hotel*
der Golftrainer, –	*golf pro*
das Informationsmaterial, -materialien	informational material
klettern	to climb
mittwochs	Wednesdays
montags	Mondays
samstags	Saturdays
senden	to send, transmit
die Ski- und Snowboardschule, -n	*skiing and snowboarding school*
die Sportreise, -n	*sports trip*
der Sportreiseveranstalter, –	*sports trip organizer*
der Tageskurs, -e	one-day course
der Tagesskipass, ¨e	day pass for skiing
das Tischtennis (nur Singular)	*table tennis, ping pong*
das Top-Angebot, -e	*top offer*
zu·faxen	*to fax to someone*
zu·mailen	*to e-mail to someone*
zu·senden	*to transmit/send to someone*

Seite 54 — page 54

Seite 54	page 54
der Absatz, ¨e	*paragraph*
der Alltag (nur Singular)	everyday life
außer	beyond, beside
der Begriff, -e	*notion, concept*
besteigen, er hat bestiegen	*to climb*
Betrieb: außer Betrieb	service: out of service

entfernt	distanced, separated
der Expertentipp, -s	*expert tip*
der Extremsportler, –	*extreme athlete*
hoch·gehen, er ist hochgegangen	*to go up high*
die Kniebeuge, -n	*knee bend*
die Laufgruppe, -n	*running group*
die Liegestütze, -n	*push-up*
das Mitglied, -er	member
normalerweise	normally
radeln	*to bike, cycle, pedal*
reagieren	to react
reichen	here: *to suffice*
selbstverständlich	of course, it's understood
umradeln	*to pedal around*

Seite 55 — page 55

ab·stufen	*to graduate, rank in importance*
aus·drücken	*to express*
darum	*here:* about it
das Interesse, -n	interest
das Präpositionaladverb, -adverbien	*prepositional adverb*
der Vokal, -e	*vowel*
womit	with what
worum	*here:* about what
wovon	*here:* of what

Seite 56 — page 56

der Bergsteiger, –	*mountain climber*
das Elbsandsteingebirge (nur Singular)	*the sandstone mountains of the Elbe River*
der Felsen, –	*cliff*
das free climbing (nur Singular)	*free climbing*
das Gebirge, –	mountain range
der Gipfel, –	*summit*
das Hilfsmittel, –	*help materials*
das Jahrhundert, -e	*century*
das Klettergebiet, -e	*climbing region*
die Kletterregel, -n	*climbing rule*
die Klettertechnik, -en	*climbing technique*
der Kletterweg, -e	*climbing path*
der Körper, –	body
meistbesucht	*most visited*
die Modesportart, -en	*type of sport that is in fashion*
sächsisch	Saxon
der Sandstein, -e	*sandstone*
der Sandsteinfelsen, –	*sandstone cliff*
das Seil, -e	*sail*
der Stein, -e	stone
südöstlich	*southeastern*
Tschechien (nur Singular)	*Czech Republic*
überprüfen	*to recheck, verify*

Seite 57 — page 57

amerikanisch	*American*
der Bergsteigerkollege, -n	*mountain climbing colleague*
die Chemiefirma, -firmen	*chemical company*
das Detail, -s	*detail*
erfolgreich	*successful*
die Freiklettertechnik, -en	*free climbing technique*
der Fußballer, –	*footballer, soccer player*
der Kletterer, –	*climber*
die Nationalmannschaft, -en	*national team*
der Sportler, –	*athlete*
die Vereinigten Staaten (nur Plural)	*United States*
die Weltmeisterschaft, -en	*world championship*

Arbeitsbuch — Workbook

Seite 122 — page 122

kämmen (sich)	*to comb*

Seite 123 — page 123

um·ziehen (sich), er hat (sich) umgezogen	to change clothes

Seite 125 — page 125

der Kinofilm, -e	cinematic film
die Sommerferien (nur Plural)	summer break

Seite 127 — page 127

Halt!	*Stop!*
das Kartenspielen (nur Singular)	*playing cards*
der Regenschirm, -e	umbrella
die Sportschau (nur Singular)	*sports show*
die Vorderseite, -n	*front page*

Seite 128 — page 128

die Fußball-Saison, -s	*football/soccer season*
das Handballspiel, -e	*handball game*
der Kuss, ¨-e	kiss

Seite 129 — page 129

das Silbenrätsel, –	*game based on syllables of words*
der Skikurs, -e	*skiing course*
der Skilehrer, –	*skiing instructor*
der Skipass, ¨-e	*skiing pass*

Seite 130 — page 130

das Abenteuer, –	*adventure*
das All-Inkusive-Angebot, -e	*all-inclusive package*
die Berghütte, -n	*mountain hut*

deutsch-böhmisch	*German-Bohemian*
entdecken	to discover
das Erzgebirge (nur Singular)	*the Erz Mountains*
die Ferienregion, -en	*vacation region*
das Flair (nur Singular)	*flair*
das Freizeitangebot, -e	*freetime offer/package*
das Fußball-Camp, -s	*football/soccer camp*
der Golf- und Tennisplatz, ¨-e	*golf and tennis court*
der Golfkurs, -e	*golf instruction*
die Golfschule, -n	*golf school*
die Grenze, -n	border, limit
der Hip Hop (nur Singular)	*hip hop*
die Internetanzeige, -n	*internet ad*
die Kletter-Tour, -en	*climbing tour*
der Lift, -e	lift
die Mountain-Bike-Tour, -en	*mountain bike tour*
der Profi, -s	*professional*
der Saisonpreis, -e	*seasonal price*
das Skigebiet, -e	*skiing region*
die Ski-Hütte, -n	*ski hut*
der Ski-Spaß (nur Singular)	*fun skiing*
der Sommer-Bergspaß (nur Singular)	*summer fun in the mountains*
der Tanzlehrer, –	*dance instructor*
die Unterbringung (nur Singular)	*accommodation, housing*
das Wellness-Angebot, -e	*wellness offer/package*
das Wellness-Hotel, -s	*wellness hotel*

Seite 131 — page 131

der Fitness-Tipp, -s	*fitness tip*
freitags	Fridays

Seite 132 — page 132

sonnabends	Saturdays (northern German)

1 Reflexive verbs *(Reflexive Verben)*

examples

*Ich kann **mich** nicht konzentrieren.* *– Du solltest **dich** ein bisschen ausruhen.*	I can't concentrate. – You should rest a little.
*Er fühlt **sich** müde, und sie fühlt **sich** auch nicht wohl.*	He feels tired and she doesn't feel well, either.
*Wir ernähren **uns** gesund.* *– Ja, aber ihr bewegt **euch** zu wenig.*	We eat well. – Yeah, but you don't move enough.
*Die Kinder duschen **sich** jeden Morgen.*	The children shower every morning.
*Setzen Sie **sich** doch!*	Sit down!

Reflexive verbs are verbs for which the verb's subject and object are the same person or thing. English reflexive verbs use reflexive pronouns ending in -self or -selves and as such are really easy to identify. German reflexive verbs also use reflexive pronouns, but their use is far more prevalent than in English. In the examples above, you can see that English often does not use a reflexive verb to express the same meaning as in German.

examples

reflexive	not reflexive
Er ärgert sich.	*Er ärgert seinen Bruder.*
Ich** ziehe **mich an.	*Ich ziehe die Kinder an.*

Notice that the verb "to aggravate", *ärgern,* can also be made reflexive in order to express what we describe in English as getting upset. Likewise, while in English, we "get dressed", one either dresses oneself or someone else in German. Returning then to the first examples above, note that concentrating is a transitive action in German; either one concentrates something (a solution, a beam of light) or oneself (i.e., one's attention), or one rests something as opposed to resting oneself; similarly, one either moves something (a piece on a chessboard, a limb, etc.) or moves oneself (an action which English speakers consider intransitive).

Additionally, there is another case where German will often make a verb reflexive where we would not: to express the idea of the subject and verb doing the action to **each other**, German will often make this reflexive: ***Wir sehen uns** bald wieder.* (We'll see each other again soon.)

This rationale will probably not make a lot of sense at first, so when learning reflexive verbs, concentrate on them as vocabulary items first, and over time, the logic of making them reflexive will become clearer.

The reflexive pronoun accompanying the verb is the same as the accusative personal pronouns in the first and second person (see *Schritte international 2*, Chapter 14), while the third person, both singular and plural, have their own pronoun (*sich*).

2 Verbs with prepositional complements *(Verben mit Präposition)*

examples with accusative

*Ich **warte auf** dich.*	I'm waiting for you.
*Sie **kümmert sich um** den Garten.*	She looks after the garden.
*Er **beschwert sich** immer **über** seinen Chef.*	He's always complaining about his boss.

examples with dative

*Ich **treffe mich** am Samstag **mit** einem Kollegen.*	I'm meeting with a colleague on Saturday.
*Anna **träumt** oft **von** ihrem Urlaub.*	Anna often dreams of her vacation.
*Wir möchten gern **mit** Ihnen **sprechen**.*	We'd really like to speak with you.

In German, as in English, there are verbs which need prepositions to complete their meaning. In German, some of these prepositions require accusative objects, and some require dative objects. Though both languages have verbs with prepositional complements, the complements do not often correspond from one language to another, as you can see in several examples above. Thus, it is imperative that you learn German verbs with their complements as well as the case they require. Prepositions are always culturally specific and not usually "logical", so in this regard, there is no shortcut for straight rote learning and repetition.

Some verbs can have more than one possible complement, such as *sich freuen*.
When this verb combines with *auf*, it has an entirely different meaning that when it combines with *über*: *Sich freuen auf* refers to looking forward to a future event or condition, or being happy about something to come, while *sich freuen über* indicates that the subject is happy about something current.

examples

*Ich **freue mich** schon **auf** das Wochenende.*	I'm already looking forward to the weekend.
*Ich **freue mich über** die gute Fußball-Saison.*	I'm happy about the good football/soccer season.

In German, the preposition accompanying the verb *helfen* is *bei* and not *mit*:

*Kannst du mir **bei** den Hausaufgaben **helfen**?*	Can you help me with the homework?

3 Prepositional adverbs *(Präpositionaladverbien)*

examples

*Hast du Lust **auf Tischtennis**?*	Do you feel like playing tennis?
*– Nein, **darauf** habe ich überhaupt keine Lust.*	– No, I have absolutely no interest in that.
***Worauf** hast du denn Lust?*	What are you interested in?
*– **Auf** eine Partie Uno.*	– A round of Uno.
***Woran** denkst du?*	What are you thinking about?
*– **An** die Prüfungen.*	– The exams.
*Ja, **daran** muss ich auch immer denken.*	Yeah, I keep thinking about them all the time, too.
***Womit** arbeitet ihr im Deutschkurs?*	What are you working with in German class?
*– **Mit** Schritte international.*	– *Schritte international.*
***Damit** arbeiten wir auch.*	We work with it, too.

Just as pronouns are used to avoid repetition of nouns, often it is preferable to do the same with objects of prepositions. In the case of inanimate prepositional complements (things instead of people), instead of using a personal pronoun, the prefix *da-* is attached to the front of the preposition. If the preposition begins with a vowel, an *-r-* is added to make pronunciation easier (*da + auf → darauf*, *da + an → daran*).

When asking a question, instead of *da-*, the prefix *wo-* is added to the preposition that would complement the verb (*worauf? woran? womit?* etc.). This is in stark contrast to common English usage, where we would ask the question using *what* and put the preposition at the end of the phrase. Even if the most colloquial German speech, that pattern (a lone preposition at the end of a phrase) never occurs. Sometimes, in speech, one hears the following constructions:

Mit was arbeitet ihr? (instead of *Womit ...?*)
An was denkst du? (instead of *Woran ...?*)

Remember that these prepositional adverbs, these compounds with *da-* and *wo-*, can only be used to refer to inanimate objects. When referring to a person, a personal pronoun is still used: *María interessiert sich für Antonio.* ***An wen*** *denkt sie? Sie denkt viel* ***an ihn****.*

4 Temporal adverbs: *morgens, montags*

examples

Ich esse ***morgens*** *gern Brötchen.*	In the mornings, I like to eat rolls.
Abends *esse ich oft Salat.*	In the evenings, I often eat salad.
Montags *und* ***mittwochs*** *spiele ich Tennis.*	Mondays and Wednesdays, I play tennis.

In English, we differentiate between days of the week in a prepositional phrase (on Monday) to denote one particular day, and adverbs (Mondays) to denote recurring activities. German uses the same distinction; to create the adverbial form, an *-s* is added to the end of the day's name, just like English, but in German, it is written in lower case.

5 Translate into English.

a *Ärger dich doch nicht so!* ....!

– Doch ich ärgere mich. Der Bus ist schon ....

wieder nicht gekommen! ....!

b *Pedro sollte sich mehr bewegen. In der* ....

letzten Zeit ist er ein bisschen dick geworden. ....:

– Ja, er sollte ein bisschen joggen. ....:

c *Woran denkst du gerade?* ....?

– An die Ferien. Ich möchte dieses Jahr wieder ....

nach Ecuador (fahren). ....:

– Ja, das war wirklich schön. ....:

d *Ich interessiere mich für einen Golfkurs.* ....:

Ich bin Anfänger. Können Sie mir da etwas ....

empfehlen? ....?

– Ja, wir haben gerade ein Top-Angebot. ....:

6 **Translate into German.**

a Don't wait for me. I still have to change clothes. ....

– Fine, we'll see (each other) at Marta's then. .... *dann* .... *Marta.*

b Do you remember Mr. Wagner? .... *Herrn* .... ?

– Yes, we met at the Four Seasons Hotel in New York, didn't we? .... *nicht?*

c What do you do when you can't concentrate? .... ?

– I go for a walk. ....

d Sundays, we like to sleep for a long time. .... *lange.*

– Oh yeah? We don't. We always get up early. ....

Listening and Pronunciation

Pronunciation of <r>

interessieren ● *Regen* ● *Treffen*

The German <r> at the beginning of a syllable is pronounced like the French <r>. It is not rolled on the tongue, like the Spanish <r>, but instead originates at the back of the mouth. The closest approximation is gargling without water. As one goes farther south in Germany, as well as into Austria, the sound moves more forward in the mouth.

Stress in prepositional adverbs

woran ● *daran*
worum ● *darum*

For purposes of learning right now, the syllabic stress on *da-* and *wo-* compounds falls on the first syllable. For purposes of emphasis, that may vary, but as a general rule, it is safest to always stress the first syllable.

Stress on sentence elements: reflexive pronouns

Du bewegst dich zu wenig.

Unless the reflexive pronoun must be stressed to contrast against a prior statement, it is not stressed, since it does not provide the most essential information.

Familiarity and Understanding

It's wild!
Protected areas in northern Germany

In Europe, there are few wild areas, even counting national parks. The fourteen national parks in Germany comprise only 2.6% of its total land area. The Bavarian Forest was the first declared protected zone in 1970. The smallest, the Jasmund National Park (3000 hectares or about 7400 acres) is the largest in the former East Germany, on the island of Rügen in the Baltic Sea, and its unique landscape of Cretaceous-era rock formations was made famous by the Romantic painter Caspar David Friedrich.

As in many other parts of the world, the hand of man has helped erode part of this landscape, where rocks fall vertically from the famous chalk cliffs into the sea. In the late nineteenth and early twentieth centuries, mining of the chalk from the cliffs weakened their structures until they were named a *Naturschutzgebiet* (nature preserve area) in 1929. Conservation efforts were further threatened when the area became a huge draw for tourists after the Wall fell, and in 1990, the area was named a national park in order to better preserve it.

The North Sea is home to Germany's largest national park, or more accurately, the three Wadden Sea National Parks (*Nationalpark Wattenmeer*) in three federal states with shoreline adjoining along the North Sea. Along this shore, low tide exposes extensive mud flats that were created by storm tides between 1100 and 1500 A.D. This unique landscape is not only a protected natural park network, but also a biosphere reserve which receives additional protection from UNESCO. The entire Wadden Sea stretches from Holland along the western coast of Germany, from Lower Saxony along Hamburg state and on to Schleswig-Holstein, and continues along the Danish coast. In all, the Wadden Sea stretches along 500 km (310 miles) of coastline. These wetlands are home to remarkable biodiversity: among the more than 3000 species living there are seals, whales and herring. Some 250 species are unique to this landscape where one of the local recreational activities are *Wattwanderungen*, i.e. hiking through the low tide.

On October 11, 1634, during the Thirty Years' War, there was a terrible storm on the North Sea which unleashed what came to be known as the Burchardi Flood. It formed the present-day appearance of Schleswig-Holstein's western coast destroyed an island then called Strand. Today, the two remaining sections of what was once Strand are two separate islands known now as Nordstrand and Pellworm, and the islet of Nordstrandischmoor.

A islet or holm (known in German as a *Hallig*) is a small island with no protective levees that can disappear during flooding. To protect themselves, residents often make their homes on a *Warft* (artificial hill). A *Hallig* has no drinking water wells. There are ten such *Halligen* in the North Sea. On the smallest of them, Süderoog (0.60 sq km), there are only 2 inhabitants, while fewer than 120 live on the largest. In the past, there were many more *Halligen* but some have disappeared from the map, literally swallowed by the sea.

Lessons from the top of the world

Around the globe, only fourteen mountains surpass 8000 meters in height (26,247 feet). Among the five people who have so far reached the summits of all fourteen so-called "eight-thousanders" without oxygen is one man born in 1944 into a German-speaking minority in the Tyrolean region of northern Italy, Reinhold Messner. Messner has been challenging summits and other inhospitable landscapes throughout his life. Between mid-November 1989 and February 1990, he crossed Antarctica on foot, covering 2800 km (1740 miles) in three months, walking in temperatures as low as –40 °C and winds reaching 150 kph (93 mph). Another landscape, the Gobi desert in Mongolia, caught his attention in 2004, when he and his son hiked 2000 km (1243 miles) across it.

Messner has said that mountaineering is closer to art than to sport, and that climbing mountains is as useless as are the fine arts. Messner has no use for sophisticated equipment and prefers to carry the minimum necessary to cope with nature's challenges. In seeking to experience Nature as it is, not as anyone would have it be, he uses no hooks, supplemental oxygen, or mobile telephones.
Messner first achieved worldwide fame in 1970, when he and his brother Günther climbed the Nanga Parbat in Pakistan. Though they reached the summit, Günther died during the descent and Reinhold was accused of sacrificing his brother for his own success. Remains found in 2003, however, demonstrated that Günther died in a fall resulting from a misstep as Reinhold had always maintained. In January 2007, charges brought based upon a supposed diary supplied by two other members of the Messners' team were dismissed when it was determined that the diary was a forgery.

Reinhold Messner has also served as a member of the European parliament, not surprisingly as a member of the Green Party.
"Our lives are more formed by our awareness than by circumstances," he says. "Anyone who does not live experience remains stalled. Anyone who lives second hand only consumes. Nothing has given me more awareness than the landscape and its resonance in my soul."
Currently, Messner has opened the Messner Mountain Museum and has established the Messner Mountain Foundation that provides aid to mountain villages around the world.

Historical Fragments

Prussia

At the mouth of the Vistula river on the Baltic coast of what is now Poland, a small duchy was formed in 1525 which later became the seat of the unified German state: Prussia.
As Protestants, the Duchy was subjected to numerous invasions during the Thirty Years War but managed through shrewd forging of alliances and relationships to build the Duchy into the well-organized and eventually absolutist Kingdom of Prussia.

This kingdom openly welcomed emigrants, among them the Huguenots, Protestants who were persecuted in France. They came in tens of thousands to populate Prussia in the seventeenth century. To a large extent, they were qualified individuals who contributed greatly to the economy of the emerging Prussia (which by this point was more Brandenburg than Prussia, but the name of the Duchy had carried over to the expanding Kingdom), and by the end of the seventeenth century, every third inhabitant of Berlin spoke French.

In 1701, Prussia became a significant power within the Holy Roman Empire. *Friedrich der Große* (Frederick the Great, 1740–1786) carried out several wars against Maria Theresia of Austria for Silesia. The last of these wars was the so-called Seven Years War (known in the United States as the French and Indian War) from 1756 to 1763. All European states were involved in this war, making it effectively the first world war: Britain fought with Prussia against France and Spain, and these two states were also at war with overseas colonies in the Americas and Asia, while Russia and Sweden battled Prussia in Eastern Europe. In the North American colonies, Great Britain defeated France, who lost Canada and the Northwest Territories, Spain lost Florida, and Prussia won Silesia from Austria.

With this victory, the foundation was laid for what historians term German dualism, the conflict between Austria and Prussia for control of what remained of the Holy Roman Empire. This conflict would not be resolved until 1871, when the German Reich, under Prussia's leadership and dominance, was established.

Self-Evaluation

Sports and Games

When listening, I can understand (Hören)

– Simple sports reports: *„... nun zum Handball: die Deutschen Handballerinnen verlieren gegen ...“*
– Simple telephone conversations related to sports activities: *„Bieten Sie eigentlich auch Kletterkurse an?“*

In written texts, I can understand (Lesen)

– Short advertisements: *„Wandern im Erzgebirge. Natur pur auf 197 Kilometern“*
– Short texts offering health advice: *„Sie fühlen sich schwach? Sie müssen sich mehr bewegen.“*
– Short, specific texts relating to individual sports like *Freiklettern*

I can produce the following oral structures (Sprechen)

– Express a problem or dissatisfaction, give advice: *„Wenn ich mich nicht konzentrieren kann, dann gehe ich spazieren ...“*
– Talk about my interests, ask about others' interest, and react: *„Interessieren Sie sich für ...? / Haben Sie Lust auf ...“*
– Get information by phone on services: *„Ich interessiere mich für .../ Könnten Sie mir Informationsmaterial zusenden?“*
– Understand advice and opinions: *„Das passt / Das stimmt nicht.“*

I can produce the following written texts (Schreiben)

– A “sports agenda”: *„Montags gehe ich schwimmen, dienstags ...“*
– An e-mail discussing my sports activities
– A brief biography of a famous athlete

Kursbuch	Textbook
Seite 58	**page 58**
das Abitur (nur Singular)	final exam after the 12th class of the Gymnasium
die Abschlussprüfung, -en	*final exam of a course of study*
arm	poor
die Biologie (nur Singular)	biology
blöd	*stupid, silly, daft*
das Fach, ¨er	subject
faul	lazy
fleißig	industrious, hard-working
das Gymnasium, Gymnasien	university-preparatory secondary school
intelligent	intelligent
die Karriere, -n	*career*
die Note, -n	grade, mark
reich	rich
das Zeugnis, -se	report card
das Zwischenzeugnis, -se	progress report
Seite 59	**page 59**
anscheinend	apparently
dass	(conjunction) that
froh	happy
das Mathelernen (nur Singular)	learning math
recht: recht haben	right, correct, to be correct
die Sorge, -n	worry, care
das Verhalten (nur Singular)	behavior, reaction
Seite 60	**page 60**
anders herum	*the other way around*
der Anwalt, ¨e	lawyer
die Bankkauffrau, -en	*bank executive (female)*
die Bäuerin, -nen	farmer (female)
der Bauernhof, ¨e	*farm*
die Buchhändlerin, -nen	*book dealer (female)*
die Lehre, -n	apprenticeship
der Pilot, -en	pilot
die Schneiderin, -nen	*tailor (female), seamstress*
Seite 61	**page 61**
der Erfolg, -e	success
Seite 62	**page 62**
der/die Auszubildende, -n	apprentice
das Berufskolleg, -s	*trade school course of study*
die Berufsschule, -n	trade school
die Chemie (nur Singular)	chemistry
die Erdkunde (nur Singular)	*earth science*
die Fachhochschule, -n	*university-level institution granting Diplom degrees and higher in specific fields of study (usually technical)*
die Fachoberschule, -n	*city college, technical school*
freiwillig	voluntary
die Gesamtschule, -n	comprehensive secondary school
die Grundschule, -n	elementary school (classes 1 to 4)
das Handwerk (nur Singular)	*handwork*
hassen	to hate
die Hauptschule, -n	secondary school (leading to occupational training)
die Krippe, -n	*child care center*
das Lieblingsfach, ¨er	*favorite subject*
der Lieblingslehrer, –	*favorite teacher*
der Mathelehrer, –	math teacher
der Mechaniker, –	mechanic
die Physik (nur Singular)	physics
die Realschule, -n	secondary school (more comprehensive than Hauptschule)
das Schema, -s/Schemata	schematic
das Schulsystem, -e	*school system*
der Schulweg, -e	*path to school*
die Schulzeit, -en	*school time*
Seite 63	**page 63**
die Altersgruppe, -n	*age group*
die Angst, ¨e	fear
der Beginn (nur Singular)	*beginning*
die Beratung, -en	advising, counseling
das Bewerbungsschreiben, –	*letter of application*
bluten	to bleed
die CD-ROM, -s	CD-ROM
chancenreich	rich in chances or opportunities
der Computer-Club, -s	*computer club*
die Computer-Putzaktion, -en	*computer clean-up mission*
die Datei, -en	computer file
das Denktraining, -s	*training of reasoning and thinking skills*
der Einblick, -e	*view inside*
die Einführung, -en	introduction
die Erfahrung, -en	experience
der Erste-Hilfe-Kurs, -e	*first aid course*
der Fernsehfilm, -e	TV movie/film
die Festplatte, -n	hard drive
flirten	*to flirt*
das Frühjahr, -e	spring
der Frühjahrsputz (nur Singular)	*spring cleaning*
fürchten	to fear
das Gehirn, -e	*brain*
das Gehirn-Jogging (nur Singular)	*"brain jogging," exercise for the brain*
die Gesellschaft, -en	society, company
halten, du hältst, er hält, er hat gehalten	*here:* to keep, preserve
der Handgriff, -e	*technique, maneuver*
herein·tanzen	*to dance in*
der Konflikt, -e	*conflict*
das Konflikttraining, -s	*conflict (resolution) training*
konstruktiv	*constructive*
die Kultur (nur Singular)	culture

die Lohnverhandlung, -en	*wage negotiation*
löschen	*to erase, delete*
mit·tanzen	*to dance with/along*
der Notarzt, ¨e	*emergency physician*
die Notsituation, -en	*emergency situation*
der Ordner, –	*document binder*
die Politik (nur Singular)	politics
die Rhetorik (nur Singular)	*rhetoric*
säubern	*to clean*
speichern	to save/store
spielerisch	*playful*
der Streit, -s	argument
der Tanz, ¨e	dance
die Technik, -en	technique
teil·nehmen, du nimmst teil, er nimmt teil, er hat teilgenommen	to participate
der Umgang (nur Singular)	*contact, interaction*
um·gehen, er ist umgegangen	*to deal with*
verletzt	injured
vermeiden, er hat vermieden	*to avoid*
die Voraussetzung, -en	condition (set in advance)
das Vorstellungsgespräch, -e	*introductory interview*
das Weiterbildungszentrum, -zentren	*continuing education center*
der Workshop, -s	*workshop*
die Zelle, -n: graue Zellen	*cell: gray cells (in gray matter)*

Seite 64 — page 64

die Bar, -s	bar (where drinks are served)
die Berufsfee, -n	*career fairy*
die Berufsfinderin, -nen	*career finder (female)*
die Berufswahl (nur Singular)	*choice of profession*
der Biologe, -n	*biologist*
erfüllen	to fulfill
die Fee, -n	*fairy*
die Kapitänin, -nen	*female captain*
konkret	*concrete*
der Rockstar, -s	*rock star*
der Schritt, -e	step
der Tänzer, –	*dancer*
tatsächlich	in fact
der Traumberuf, -e	*dream profession*
unglücklich	unhappy
der Weinbauer, -n	*vintner*
weiter·gehen, es ist weitergegangen	to go on, to continue
der Wunschberuf, -e	*profession one wishes for*

Seite 65 — page 65

der Berufsweg, -e	*career path*
das Gefühl, -e	feeling

Seite 66 — page 66

die Aggression, -en	*aggression*
die Akrobatik (nur Singular)	*acrobatics*
das Ensemble, -s	*ensemble*
entstehen, es ist entstanden	to come into existence
der Licht- und Videoeffekt, -e	*light and video effect*
die Presse (nur Singular)	press (media)
die Probe, -n	*test, rehearsal*
das Publikum (nur Singular)	audience
rufen	to call
die Schwebebahn, -en	*suspended railway*
das Tanztheater, –	*dance theater*
das Theaterstück, -e	*theatrical piece*
unzufrieden	dissatisfied
weiter·kommen, er ist weitergekommen	to come further along

Seite 67 — page 67

begegnen	to encounter
die Choreographin, -nen	*female choreographer*
erarbeiten	*to develop*
der Fensterputzer, –	*window cleaner*
inzwischen	in the meantime
der Lebensgefährte, -n	*life partner*
die Leiterin, -nen	*female leader (of a department or group)*
die Tanzausbildung, -en	*education in dance*
der Tanzschritt, -e	*dance step*
das Tanztheaterstück, -e	*theatrical dance work*

Arbeitsbuch — Workbook

Seite 134 — page 134

das Skateboard, -s (fahren)	*skateboard*
der Tourismus (nur Singular)	*tourism*

Seite 135 — page 135

der Sportverein, -e	*sports club*

Seite 136 — page 136

der Mathematiker, –	*mathematician*

Seite 138 — page 138

die Fußballmannschaft, -en	*football/soccer team*
mit·spielen	*to play along/with*
der Wecker, –	alarm clock

Seite 139 — page 139

der Hauptschulabschluss, ¨e	*graduation from Hauptschule*
das Kursbuch, ¨er	*course book, textbook*
der Sportunterricht (nur Singular)	*sports class/instruction*
zusammen·arbeiten	to work together, cooperate

Seite 141	page 141
das Bewerbungsgespräch, -e	*job interview*
das Computerprogramm, -e	*computer program*
die Englischkenntnisse (nur Plural)	English language skills

Seite 142	page 142
an·melden (sich)	to register (oneself)
der Druckbuchstabe, -n	*printed letter*
das Fachabitur (nur Singular)	*vocational diploma*
der Firmenchef, -s	*company boss*
das Gasthaus, ¨-er	*inn*
das Geburtsland, ¨-er	country of one's birth
das Inland (nur Singular)	domestic territory
der Koch, ¨-e	*cook*
der Lehrling, -e	*apprentice*
der Maschinenbau (nur Singular)	*mechanical engineering*
der Personenwagen, –	*passenger vehicle*
die Produktion, -en	production
die Serie, -n	*series*
der Studienabschluss, ¨-e	*conclusion of a course of study; graduation*
übernehmen, du übernimmst, er übernimmt, er hat übernommen	to take over
der/die Vorstandsvorsitzende, -n	*chair of the board of directors*
das Weltunternehmen, –	*global business/business venture*
der Werkzeugmacher, –	*toolmaker*
zurück·senden	to send back

Seite 143	page 143
flexibel	*flexible*
die Fremdsprachenkenntnisse (nur Plural)	*foreign language skills*
Jura (nur Singular)	*law (study of)*
die Theatergruppe, -n	*theater group*

Seite 144	page 144
das Schulfach, ¨-er	*school subject*

1 The *Präteritum* of modal verbs *(Modalverben: Präteritum)*

examples

*Was **wollten** Sie als Kind werden?*	As a child, what did you want to be?
***Konntest** du nicht etwas früher kommen?*	Couldn't you come earlier?
*Frau Emmerich, Sie **sollten** doch ein Hotelzimmer reservieren, haben Sie das schon gemacht?*	Ms. Emmerich, you were supposed to reserve a hotel room, did you do that already?
*Ich **durfte** zu Hause nicht viel fernsehen.*	I wasn't allowed to watch much TV at home.
***Musstet** ihr früher auch immer den Müll runterbringen?*	Did you always have to take out the trash too?

In Chapter 8 of *Schritte international 2,* we became acquainted with the *Präteritum* of the verbs *haben* and *sein,* and we saw that all the forms of *haben* add the *-t-* (followed by an *-e-*), as a sort of pattern for the *Präteritum* of weak verbs.
The modal verbs follow the same pattern.

Compare:

ich	*hat-te*	*woll-te*
du	*hat-test*	*woll-test*
er/sie	*hat-te*	*woll-te*
wir	*hat-ten*	*woll-ten*
ihr	*hat-tet*	*woll-tet*
sie/Sie	*hat-ten*	*woll-ten*

Modal verbs that have an *Umlaut* in their infinitive drop it in the *Präteritum.*

infinitive	Präteritum
müssen	*ich musste*
können	*ich konnte*
dürfen	*ich durfte*

examples

Ich möchte kein Brot mehr, danke.	I would not like any more bread, thanks.
– Hier, nimm doch noch etwas.	– Here, take some!
Hey, ich wollte doch kein Brot mehr!	Hey, I didn't want any more bread!

For the subjunctive verb *„möchten"*, the *Präteritum* of *wollen* is used for past time.
The form *mochte-* corresponds to the verb *mögen.* Remember that *mögen* does not express desire but rather liking or disliking. *(Ich mag keinen Fisch. / Ich mag die neue Kollegin.)*

2 The conjunction *dass (Konjunktion: dass)*

examples

Findest du Noten wichtig?	Do you think grades are important?
*Findest du, **dass** Noten wichtig sind?*	Do you think that grades are important?
Eine gute Ausbildung ist wichtig.	A good education is important.
*Es ist wichtig, **dass** man eine gute Ausbildung hat.*	It's important that one get a good education.

The conjunction *dass* begins a subordinate clause. It is equivalent to the English conjunction *that* (not to be confused with the demonstrative pronoun *that*).

examples *Papa meint, **dass** ich faul **bin**.* — Dad thinks that I am lazy.
*Ich glaube, **dass** Kurt zu streng **ist**.* — I think that Kurt is too strict.
*Simon ist froh, **dass** Maria da **ist**.* — Simon is happy that Maria is there.

*(Es ist) schade, **dass** du nicht kommen **kannst**.* — (It's a) pity that you can't come.

Statements with *dass* are often used to express an opinion or an emotion.
As in English, a speaker has the option to leave the *dass* out of the statement, but the two clauses must still be separated by a comma:

Papa meint, ich bin faul. — Dad thinks I'm lazy.

3 Translate into English.

a *Ihr solltet doch die Übung 4 machen!* ....!

– Oh, das haben wir vergessen! ....!

b *Herr Burli, wollten Sie heute nicht um* ....

3 Uhr gehen? ....?

– Ja, aber ich muss noch das Programm ....

fertig machen. ....:

c *Glauben Sie, dass man auch mit schlechten* ....

Noten noch Erfolg im Beruf haben kann? ....?

– Da bin ich sicher! ....!

d *Findest du es schlimm, dass Bob sitzen* ....

geblieben ist? ....?

– Ich finde es eigentlich nicht so schlimm, ...

aber sein Vater ist sauer. ....:

4 Translate into German.

a My mother wanted to be a teacher, but ....

she wasn't allowed to study at the ....

university. ....:

b Shouldn't Anna take this Excel class? ....?

– Yes, but it was on Mondays and Wed- Ja, aber der ....

nesdays and she couldn't do it then. und da ....:

c	I'm very happy that Tony found a	....
	job at Mercedes.	....
	– Yeah, he was lucky, but he also speaks	– Ja, er hat ....
	good German, doesn't he?	.... auch gut .... , ... ?
d	Excuse me, I wanted to ask something:	....
	have you registered for the class „Die	....
	Kunst des Flirtens"?	.... ?
	– Yeah, why?	.... ?
e	As a child, I always had to clean up my	Als Kind ....
	room and help with the shopping.	.... beim Einkaufen ....
	– Yeah, me too.	....

Listening and Pronunciation

The pronunciation of <-ig>

wenig ● *zwanzig*

The pronunciation of the final <-ig>, in standard German, sounds like <ich>.
Nevertheless, in some southern dialects as well as in parts of Austria and Switzerland, it is pronounced [-ik].

The consonants <f> and <v>

Frühstück ● *Verein*
Anfang ● *Vorname*
Brief ● *Vater*

The letters <f> and <v> have the same sound, the [f] sound, in all words of German origin. Only in words of foreign derivation does the <v> sound like our <v>.

The consonants <v> and <w>

Vater ● *Wasser*

Just as Germans learning English tend to reverse these sounds, so do we tend to when learning German. Again, the <v> is equivalent to [f], while the German <w> is the same as our <v>.

Familiarity and Understanding

Was Hänschen nicht lernt, lernt Hans nimmermehr?
(What little Hans doesn't learn, Hans will never learn?)

In Germany as in the United States, education is the responsibility of the states and not of the federal government. There are some private schools in Germany, but they are relatively few (2,600 compared to 36,000 public), meaning that German education is practically all public. Compulsory education varies from one state to another, most of them prescribing 9 years. In some states, the requirement includes vocational training if pupils leave school at age 16.

Children may attend kindergarten from ages three to six. After kindergarten, their primary education begins. In some states, children have four years of primary school, in others six. Then the parents decide, usually upon the recommendation of the primary school, whether their son or daughter will follow one of these three options:

Hauptschule (of which there are more than 5,000 in Germany) provides general and primarily practical education (from 5th to 9th or 10th grade, which in the United States would chronologically be the end of sophomore year of high school) allowing the student at age 16 to either seek work or begin vocational training in one of the *Berufsschulen* (vocational schools), as described in *Schritte international 2*, Chapter 1.

Those who opt for the *Realschule* (of which there are about 3,000) receive a general education that is broader than that of a *Hauptschule* and is more oriented to higher professional training.

Those who wish to study beyond what we would consider the high-school level need to enter the *Gymnasium*, where students usually spend 8 years. There are about 3,000 *Gymnasien* in Germany. It was Wilhelm von Humboldt, brother of the explorer Alexander von Humboldt, who in the early 19th century, introduced the humanistic curriculum to the *Gymnasium*. Students complete *Gymnasium* with a certificate which is called the *Abitur* in Germany, the *Matura* in Austria and the *Maturität* in Switzerland.

Gesamtschulen

Alongside the traditional three-track educational system, there is an alternative model with roots in the 17th century but only fully realized in the latter part of the 20th century. In contrast to the *Realschule*, *Hauptschule* and *Gymnasium*, *Gesamtschulen* do not set students in academic programs based on what is believed to be their potential as determined at nine years of age but function more like an American high school. In the *Gesamtschule* model, students of all skill levels, inclinations and socioeconomic backgrounds attend school together. Though first proposed by Comenius and promoted by the Allied forces after World War II, the *Gesamtschulen* first really came into being in the 1970s, introduced by Social Democrats seeking to provide more equality and access to opportunity for all. Detractors, however, accustomed to decades of the three-track system, argued that highly qualified students would be hindered by others of lesser talents. Results from PISA testing have neither confirmed nor refuted such a concern, though they do show that socioeconomic factors are a greater determiner of academic success in the 800 *Gesamtschulen* across Germany than they are in the *Gymnasien*. Overall though among European countries, the German education system is showing more weakness, according to measures such as PISA.

A, B, C ... or 1, 2, 3?

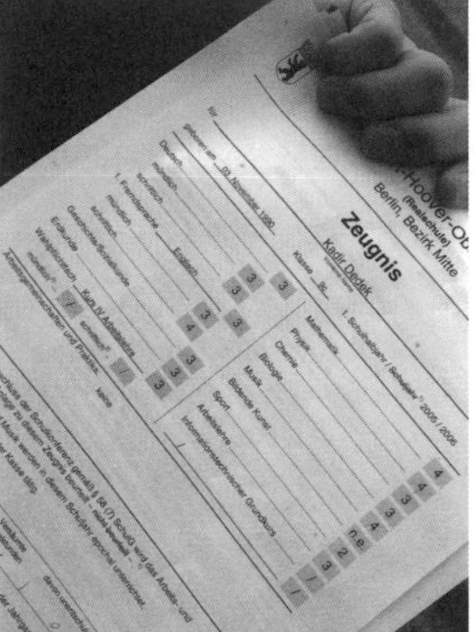

In Switzerland, there are 6 grades, with 6 being the highest like the A in the U.S. In Germany, however, it is precisely the opposite, with 6 as the lowest, and 1 being outstanding. In Austria, 5 is the worst possible grade. In Germany, a grade of 5 or 6 amounts to a suspension until a 4 is achieved.

A woman's pen is mightier than the sword

When one thinks of a pacifist, the image that comes to mind is quite likely not that of a nineteenth-century countess or a governess in a wealthy house.

Still, the woman who appears on the 2 Euro coin in Austria fits both descriptions: she is the writer, essayist and Nobel Peace Prize recipient Bertha von Suttner.

Austria can claim two female Nobel laureates: the first, in 1905, was awarded to Bertha von Suttner, and the other nearly 100 years later to author Elfriede Jelinek (*"The Pianist"*, among other novels).

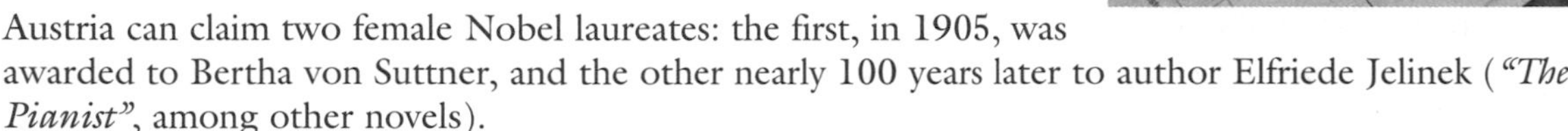

The first Nobel Peace Prize was awarded in 1901 to Henri Dunant, founder of the International Red Cross. Since Bertha von Suttner's award four years later, only nine women have since been so honored. Born Countess Kinsky in Prague in 1843 to an aristocratic but impoverished family, Bertha von Suttner took employment in 1873 as a governess at the home of the Suttner family in Vienna, where she gave language and music lessons. She fell in love with the family's son Arthur, but both families disapproved and in 1876, Arthur's mother sent her to work as a secretary and housekeeper in the home of Alfred Nobel in Paris.

She had been in Paris for barely more than a week when the King of Sweden recalled Nobel, and Bertha and Arthur married in secret. Arthur's family disowned him and they went to live in the Caucasus. It was at this time that she began writing novels. In 1877, Arthur began writing to the German press about the war between Russia and Turkey, and Bertha also wrote under a pseudonym.

In 1885, the pair returned to Vienna, were reconciled with Arthur's family and Bertha continued to write. Her most famous novel, entitled *„Die Waffen nieder!"* (Lay down your arms!) was published in 1889. For many years, it was considered the most famous anti-war work and was translated into 16 different languages.

Bertha von Suttner was firmly convinced that an international court of arbitration could avoid conflicts and wars, so in 1897 she filed a petition with the Austrian Emperor appealing for the establishment of such a court. Two years later, she participated in preparations for an international peace conference involving 26 states in The Hague. In 1902 her husband died, but Bertha continued her struggle for peace that took her to the United States for seven months, where she lectured and was received by President Theodore Roosevelt.

In 1905, she received the Nobel Peace Prize, which she had encouraged Alfred Nobel to establish. Though she saw him only twice after leaving his employment, they corresponded for the rest of Nobel's life and she is believed to have been the driving force behind his decision to establish the Prize in his will. Bertha von Suttner died of cancer in 1914, only a few weeks before the assassination of Archduke Ferdinand and his wife in Sarajevo, the incident that triggered the First World War. Though she had dedicated her life to pursuing peace, it was her homeland that triggered the greatest conflict the world had known.

Historical Fragments

The Thirty Years' War (1618–1648)

Imagine one-third of Europe's population dead from starvation or warfare, large areas of the contintent devastated, and the mouths of the Weser, Oder and Elbe rivers all controlled by foreign powers — such was Europe in 1648 at the end of the Thirty Years' War.

Though the Peace of Augsburg brought a halt to armed conflict between Catholics and German Lutherans in 1555, it did not resolve differences within the Holy Roman Empire. These continued into the following century and, in 1618, erupted into outright war across Europe, though mostly centered in what is now Germany.
When Catholic Archduke Ferdinand II of Austria became the heir apparent to the title of King of Bohemia (located in what is today the Czech Republic) the predominantly Protestant population of Bohemia went into open revolt. Although the Bohemian nobles did not stop his ascension, they did go so far as to throw Ferdinand's representatives out of a window and into a pile of horse manure. Ferdinand II was soon named the Holy Roman Emperor, which had serious consequences: though the Protestant princes of Bohemia did not want to rebel against the emperor, others did, and war ensued. The Catholics triumphed in 1620 in Bohemia, and the rebels were executed. From then on, Bohemia remained under the domination of Catholic Austria until 1918.

Elsewhere, the King of Denmark wanted to come to the aid of the German Protestants, but was defeated and his forces wiped out by Catholic troops. The Emperor's forces then occupied almost the whole of Germany to the Baltic coast. In the year 1629, the Emperor, at the zenith of his power, subjugated the Protestants.

Assessing the situation, the King of Sweden, Gustav Adolf, (Protestant but financially subsidized by the French Catholic king) saw his chance to turn Sweden into a great power. He landed his forces in Germany, defeated the Emperor's troops, and marched into Munich. Wallenstein, a Bohemian aristocrat, raised a fighting army on behalf of the Holy Roman Emperor Ferdinand II. The Swedish king Gustav Adolf fell in the battle of Lützen in 1632, yet the Swedish army continued fighting.

Only after Sweden had been defeated several times by imperial troops did France openly enter the conflict. The aim was to weaken the House of Habsburg, since this dynasty ruled both in Austria and in Spain, leaving France under threat from the east and the southwest, as well as in the north with Spanish Habsburg troops in the Netherlands.

None of the parties involved was able to decisively turn the war in its favor, and so it came to the Peace of Westphalia in 1648.

Germany had delayed its development, in all aspects, for more than a hundred years: the end of the war devastated Germany and splintered it into many small states. It created a power vacuum in Central Europe, while Holland and more of modern-day Switzerland were separated from the German Empire and became independent. France in turn became the "great power" in Europe, replacing Spain as Europe's superpower, but war dragged on between the two for another ten years until 1659.

Self-Evaluation

Education and Career

	😃	🙂	😐
When listening, I can understand (Hören)			
– Interviews on education-related topics: *„Sind Noten wirklich wichtig?“*			
– Personal information about someone's education: *„Ich war zuerst im Kindergarten, dann …“*			
– Telephone consultations on fields of academic study: *„Entschuldigung, ich suche einen Kurs …“*			
In written texts, I can understand (Lesen)			
– Advertisements of educational offerings			
– A short written interview: *„Frau Glaubitz, warum sind so viele Menschen unglücklich in ihrem Job?“*			
– An article on the professional life of someone famous *(die tanzende Königin)*			
I can produce the following oral structures (Sprechen)			
– Talk about occupations that interested me in my youth: *„Als Jugendlicher wollte ich Pilot werden. später …“*			
– State my opinion: *„Ich denke, dass … / Es ist wichtig, dass … / Gute Idee!“*			
– Give someone advice: *„Sie sollten pünktlich kommen!“*			
– Talk about an educational system and my time in school: *„Mein Lieblingsfach war Mathematik …“*			
– Discuss a set topic, i.e., *Noten in der Schule*			
– Express sentiments: *„Schade, dass … / ich bin glücklich, weil …“*			
I can produce the following written texts (Schreiben)			
– A short text on someone's academic career: *„Als Kind wollte Lars Fussballspieler werden …“*			
– Fill out forms: *Familienname: … / Vorname: …*			
– A short text on my dream job: *„In meinem Traumberuf arbeite ich als …“*			

Kursbuch	Textbook
Seite 68	**page 68**
das Altersheim, -e	senior citizens' home
der Rollstuhl, ¨e	wheelchair
das Seniorenheim, -e	*senior citizens' home*
die Wäsche (nur Singular)	laundry

Seite 69	page 69
das Familienfoto, -s	*family photo*
das Fotoalbum, -alben	*photo album*
die Fotocollage, -n	*photo collage*
die Großtante, -n	*great-aunt*
zuletzt	last of all

Seite 70	page 70
die Collage, -n	*collage*
erraten, er hat erraten	*to guess correctly*
die Geldbörse, -n	wallet
der Gutschein, -e	*credit note*
die Handcreme, -s	hand cream
der Hunde-Friseur, -e	*dog clipping style*
die Kette, -n	chain
der Knochen, –	*bone*
das Parfüm, -s	perfume
die Praline, -n	*praline, candy*
schenken	to give as a gift
der Schmuck (nur Singular)	jewelry
der Zoobesuch, -e	visit to the zoo

Seite 71	page 71
der Abschluss, ¨e	*conclusion*
der Ball, ¨e	ball
der Briefumschlag, ¨e	letter envelope
drücken	to press, push
ein·packen	to pack up
das Elfchen-Gedicht, -e	*poem comprised of eleven words*
das Geschenkpapier, -e	*gift wrapping paper*
der Mixer, –	*mixer, blender*
die Rose, -n	rose
die Schere, -n	scissors
die Schleife, -n	*ribbon*
die Schnur, ¨e	*cord, string*
der Tesafilm, -e	*Scotch™ tape*

Seite 72	page 72
der Betrag, ¨e	*amount*
die Frist, -en	length of time, term
der Geschenkgutschein, -e	*gift certificate*
gültig	valid
das Kerzenlicht (nur Singular)	*candlelight*
überraschen	to surprise
verschenken	*to give away*
der Zoo, -s	zoo

Seite 73	page 73
der Abschnitt, -e	excerpt
an·schneiden, er hat angeschnitten	to slice
die Braut, ¨e	*bride*
die Bräutigam, -e	*groom*
das Brautkleid, -er	*bridal gown*
das Brautpaar, -e	*wedding couple*
der Brautstrauß, ¨e	*bridal bouquet*
der Brautwalzer, –	*wedding waltz*
feierlich	*celebratory*
die Hochzeitsfeier, -n	*wedding celebration*
die Hochzeitstorte, -n	*wedding cake*
kirchlich	*church (adjective)*
der Ratsch (nur Singular)	*rip*
der Ringtausch (nur Singular)	*exchange of rings*
der Riss, -e	*tear, rip*
das Standesamt, ¨er	governmental office where weddings are performed
tragen, er hat getragen	to wear or carry
die Träne, -n	*teardrop*
die Trauung, -en	*marriage ceremony*
vorgestern	the day before yesterday
weinen	to cry
der Zentimeter, –	centimeter

Seite 74	page 74
der Alkohol (nur Singular)	alcohol
das Budget, -s	*budget*
dekoriert	*decorated*
die Dschungelparty, -s	*jungle party*
die Hauptsache (nur Singular)	*main thing*
die Kostümparty, -s	*costume party*
statt·finden, es hat stattgefunden	to take place
die Stimmung (nur Singular)	mood
die Strandparty, -s	*beach party*
das Straßenfest, -e	*street festival*
die Tanzparty, -s	*dance party*
telefonisch	*by telephone*
überzeugen	to convince
unterhalten (sich), du unterhältst (dich), er unterhält (sich), er hat (sich) unterhalten	to talk, chat
die Unterhaltung, -en	entertainment, amusement
verkleiden	*to dress up, disguise*

Seite 75	page 75
das Akkusativpronomen, –	*accusative pronoun*
das Dativpronomen, –	*dative pronoun*
das Objekt, -e	*object*
die Stellung, -en	position
die Syntax (nur Singular)	*syntax*
die Wichtigkeit (nur Singular)	*importance*

Seite 76	page 76
das Party-Thema, Themen	*party theme*

Fragebogen | Questionnaire

Seite 78 | page 78

aktuell	current
begründen	to found, establish
der Deutschfunk (nur Singular)	*German radio*
das Ereignis, -se	event
die Handballerin, -nen	*female handball player*
komplex	*complex, complicated*
die Konversation, -en	*conversation*
die Kursbeschreibung, -en	*course description*
der Milchkaffee, -s	*café au lait*
die Nachrichtenmeldung, -en	*news report*
pur	*pure, nothing but*
der Schnupperkurs, -e	*trail course*
die Vergangenheit, -en	past (time)

Seite 79 | page 79

erkundigen (sich)	to inquire about
hinter·lassen, du hinterlässt, er hinterlässt, er hat hinterlassen	*to leave behind*

Arbeitsbuch | Workbook

Seite 147 | page 147

der Satzteil, -e	*part of a sentence*

Seite 148 | page 148

das Geburtstagsgeschenk, -e	*birthday present*
das Weihnachtsfest, -e	*Christmas festival*

Seite 149 | page 149

ersetzen	*to replace*
zurück·geben, du gibst zurück, er gibt zurück, er hat zurückgegeben	to give back

Seite 150 | page 150

die Radtour, -en	*bicycle tour*

Seite 151 | page 151

ein·fallen, dir fällt ein, ihm fällt ein, ihm ist eingefallen	to occur to someone

Seite 152 | page 152

fangen, du fängst, er fängt, er hat gefangen	to catch
das Hochzeitsessen , –	*wedding meal*
der Ring, -e	ring

Seite 153 | page 153

die Einzimmerwohnung, -en	*one-room apartment*
das Fotohandy, -s	*camera phone*
die Fotohandy-Party, -s	*camera phone party*
der Party-Test, -s	*party test*
der Pizza-Service, -s	*pizza service*
sicherlich	*surely, certainly*

1 Dative as object: possessive and indefinite articles
(Dativ als Objekt: Possessivartikel und unbestimmter Artikel)

examples

*Ina schenkt **ihrer Oma** eine Einladung ins Restaurant.*	Ina is giving her grandma an invitation to the restaurant (a meal out).*
*Ich habe **einer Freundin** mal einen Zoobesuch geschenkt.*	One time, I gave a friend a trip to the zoo.

As in English, often a verb requires both an indirect (dative) and a direct (accusative) object. When both of those objects are nouns, just like English, the indirect object will come before the direct object (dative before accusative).

examples

		dative	
m	*Geben Sie*	***Ihrem** Chef*	*bitte meine Handynummer.*
n	*Geben Sie*	***Ihrem** Kind*	*viele Vitamine.*
f	*Was schenkst du denn*	***deiner** Mutter?*	
pl	*Hans kocht*	***seinen** Kinder**n***	*heute ihr Lieblingsessen.*

Until now, you have generally seen the dative case as the case of certain prepositions, such as *seit*, *mit*, *bei*, etc. (*seit einem Jahr/mit dem Zug/bei ihrem Vater*) and as objects of certain verbs, such as *helfen* or *gefallen* (*Soll ich dir helfen? / Hat Ihnen das Buch gefallen?*). It is also the case of indirect objects, those objects which receive the direct object, and thus indirectly receive the action of the verb.

Remember that dative case markers involve the endings *-em* for masculine and neuter articles, *-er* for feminine and *-en* in the plural (with plural nouns also receiving an *-n* where possible).

examples

Wer?		***Wem?* (person)**	***Was?* (thing)**
Ina *Jan*	*schenkt* *schenkt*	*ihrer Oma* *ihr*	*eine Einladung ins Restaurant.* *Blumen.*
subject		indirect object in dative case	direct object in accusative case

In a sentence with both direct and indirect objects, the indirect object is usually a person, and the direct object is usually inanimate (a thing). The corresponding interrogatives are then *wem?* for persons and *was?* for things.

* Note that in the translation of *einladen*, the German notion of inviting someone also includes the clear unterstanding that the person inviting will also pay for everything. Thus, taking someone out for a meal is, in German, "inviting" someone.

2 Syntax: order of objects *(Syntax: Stellung der Objekte)*

examples

	dative	accusative
Ich schenke	*meiner Mutter*	*vielleicht eine Kette.*
Mein Vater schenkt	*ihr*	*wahrscheinlich (ein) Parfüm.*

As we have already seen and mentioned, when both direct and indirect objects are present, the indirect object usually comes first.

examples

	dative	accusative
Gibst du	*mir*	*das Geschenkpapier, bitte?*

	accusative	dative
Ich gebe	***es***	***dir** gleich.*

However, as it also is in English, when both the direct and indirect objects are replaced by pronouns, the accusative pronoun (direct object) will come before the dative pronoun (indirect object). In English, we need to add a preposition to the indirect object pronoun (in this case, "to you") but German does not.

3 The modal preposition: *von* + dative *(Modale Präposition: von + Dativ)*

examples

***Von wem** hast du denn den Gutschein bekommen?*
– Von meinen Kollegen.

From whom did you get the voucher? / (Who did you get the voucher from?)
– (From) my colleagues.

In addition to the use of *von* as a temporal signifier (*von neun bis dreizehn Uhr*), it also serves a modal function (from).
von requires the dative case.

Other modal prepositions are *als* and *mit*:

***Als** Kind wollte ich Krankenschwester werden.*
*Er arbeitet **als** Programmierer.*
***Mit** 14 musste ich um neun zu Hause sein.*

4 Translate into English.

a *Schenkst du deinen Großeltern etwas zum Geburtstag?* ....?
– Nicht immer. ....:

b *Finden Sie es gut, wenn man einen Gutschein schenkt?* ?

– Nein, ich finde es besser, wenn man etwas für die Person aussucht. .

c *Ich nehme die Geldbörse.* .

– Ja, gern. Soll ich sie Ihnen als Geschenk einpacken? ?

d *Wie geht denn diese blöde Übung?* ?

– Warte, ich zeige es dir. .

e *Die Blumen sind aber schön!* !

Von wem hast du sie denn bekommen? ?

– Von meinem Mann. Wir hatten gestern unseren Hochzeitstag. .

5 **Translate into German.**

a Listen, Mary, could you loan me 5 Euros? ?

I'll give them back to you tomorrow. .

– No problem! !

b David, we need the dictionary. .

– Wait, I'll give it to you right away. .

c The necklace is really beautiful! !

Who did you get it from? ?

– A girlfriend gave it to me. .

d Could you please order a coffee for me? ?

– I already ordered you one. .

e Should I write down my address for you? ?

– No thanks, you already gave it to me. .

f Mr. Peters, I heard that you got married. .

– Yes, a week ago. .

– Congratulations! !

Listening and Pronunciation

Consonant clusters

Hochzeitstag – Weihnachtsfest

Consonant clusters in German can appear quite intimidating to the student of German. Most often, they occur in compound words, so it is helpful to recognize the individual parts of the larger word (*Hoch-zeits-tag*, *Weih-nachts-fest*) and to enunciate each of them. It also helps to keep an eye out for the clusters *-tsch-* (our <ch> sound) and *-dsch-* (our <j> sound), and to recognize that when *-sh-* occurs in German, it is the combination of one syllable ending with *-s* and another beginning with *h-*, and is not equivalent to our <sh> (like *bisher*, pronounced *bis-her*).

Vocalic elision (contraction)

Wie geht's? (Wie geht es?)
Hol's dir bitte selbst! (Hol es dir bitte selbst!)
Ich hab' mir 'nen Fotoapparat gekauft. (Ich habe mir einen Fotoapparat gekauft.)
Ich geb'n dir gleich. (Ich gebe ihn dir gleich.)

Yet another characteristic common to German and English is the tendency in spoken language to drop vowels and contract words.
The vowel <e>, for example, in the pronoun „*es*", often appears as an apostrophe followed by <s>. Similarly, the diphthong <ei> at the start of indefinite articles and the *-e* on the end of first person singular verb forms also tend to be replaced by apostrophes as they are contracted in speech. The pronoun *ihn* can also be pronounced simply as <n>.

Familiarity and Understanding

German musical culture and tradition

When one thinks of German music, the first thing that comes many minds is a number of composers such as Mozart, Beethoven, Bach, Strauß, Brahms, Schubert, Schumann, Mahler, and so on.
Others think of *Weihnachtslieder*, many of which have become classic Christmas carols in our culture. In German-speaking countries, singing has always been an integral part of the culture. From early childhood, there is singing in schools, clubs and choirs, and almost everyone knows songs for any occasion: *Wanderlieder* for hiking, *Faschingslieder* for Shrovetide, or even *Trinklieder* for drinking. Musical culture and choral tradition are entrenched in Central Europe. Among the first popular songs among the general public were tunes from the operas of the Strauß family and the composer Paul Linck.

Early hits

As early as in the late 19th century, melodic songs, whether funny or sentimental, became big hits, some even known throughout the world. They were created for a mass audience and were generally frivolous, with gentle rhythms and harmonies that were fashionable at the time. By the 1940s, they came to be called *Schlager*, from the verb *schlagen*, to hit, as they basically drummed their way into the public consciousness.

German cinema, especially once sound was introduced, helped to introduce many musical styles internationally. Thus, in the 20s and 30s, unforgettable singers such as Marlene Dietrich, Zarah Leander and the vocal group the Comedian Harmonists emerged and rose to fame. Many musicians and composers were of Jewish origin, and under Nazi rule, they suffered censorship, banning and persecution. Moreover, many songs were used for propaganda purposes, as was the case throughout Europe with the success of *Lili Marleen*.

Musical variety: exoticism, folklore, songwriters, the GDR and Eurovision

The 50s had all kinds of songs to offer. Themes and musical styles were quite varied, with everything that would sell. In the 1960s and 1970s, music was globalized by mass media and, thanks to growing tourism, managed to spread even faster. One rather curious trend was the number songs about everyday topics, sung in German by foreign singers. The more accent singers displayed the better; they were considered more exotic. Songs about southern locales, love and the sun, courtesy of musical giants such as Peggy March, Cliff Richard, Nana Mouskouri, Salvatore Adamo, Julio Iglesias, and so on were enormous hits. Even in the GDR, fashionable singers were "imported" from the eastern countries, and they, too, showed evidence of Western influences and trends.

The Beatles, who got their first big break while playing in Hamburg in the late 50s and early 60s, also contributed to this phenomenon: several of their early UK and US hits were re-recorded with German-language lyrics and became huge hits in Germany.

Volksmusik was also very popular in the 50s, especially in the south, with its marked and hints of a more bucolic world. It was also popular in the GDR, despite censorship. It should come as no surprise, then, that once the Wall came down, some of the highest-rated programs on television were *Volksmusik* specials.

The emergence of *Liedermacher* (songwriters) in Germany is worthy of note as well. Marius Müller Westerhagen and Herbert Grönemeyer are prime examples of this more intellectual and socially aware genre, but there is another figure worth mentioning: GDR *Liedermacher* Wolf Biermann was equally popular in both German states, and was known for his critical stance against both Western capitalism and some of the weaknesses of the GDR socialist state. While on tour in West Germany in 1976 (with state permission) he was refused readmission to the GDR at the end of the tour and his citizenship was revoked. He lived in Hamburg and continued to record and tour, and when the Wall came down, he immediately moved back to East Germany, only to witness the end of the socialist state in the months that followed. Most recently, he completed a translation of Bob Dylan's poetry into German (a notable accomplishment, especially considering that, by his own admission, his English is not very good.)

Historical Fragments

The Protestant Reformation

Every October 31st, the Protestant regions of Germany celebrate, as it is called in the north, Reformation Day (*Reformationstag*).

On this day in 1517, the Augustine monk and theology professor *Martin Luther* published his 95 Theses in which he attacked, among other things, the Church's practice of selling indulgences ostensibly to free souls from Purgatory. Luther publicly charged that the Vatican was collecting this money for the construction of St. Peter's Basilica in Rome.

Luther was declared a heretic for making such accusations, and the Church demanded that he withdraw his theses. But in Luther's view, the Bible alone served as the foundation of Christian faith. According to Luther's theology, only Jesus Christ held supreme authority, not the Church, and only faith in God's grace could save mankind. These theses questioned the rationale of the Church's authority over believers.

Thanks to Johannes Gutenberg's printing press, developed in Mainz a few decades prior, the theses were disseminated rapidly throughout the country, and some nobles came to support Luther.

Thus Luther effectively triggered the Reformation, a period which in many ways laid the foundation for what Germany would become over the next few hundred years. Furthermore, in translating the Bible from Latin into German, he accomplished two historic landmarks: first, preaching could take place in German, and even the uneducated could understand the Bible and know for themselves that forced labor and allegiance to a sovereign were not necessarily required by God; and secondly, in his translation work, Luther created a standard of the German language for the first time, thus ushering in the modern German language.

Suddenly feeling as if they had been deceived by their rulers, peasants who now could hear the Bible in their own language revolted and where possible took up arms. The Peasant Revolt lasted from 1524 to 1526. As they were untrained in combat and often outgunned and outnumbered, many were slaughtered.

Meanwhile, Emperor Karl V was already fighting the French on one front and the Ottoman Empire on another, and in 1529 he managed to halt the Turks' advance at Vienna, but he could not bring the Protestants in Germany under control. Even after engaging his brother Ferdinand directly in the area to exercise authority, the Counterreformation was launched in 1545, only inciting further resentment and resistance among Protestant nobles. Eventually, they allied with the French (who, though Catholic, were glad to have the support in their ongoing war with Karl) in 1552, forcing the Emperor into retreat in the Netherlands.

Cuius Regio, Eius Religio

Finally, in 1555, Karl V was forced to yield: in the Peace of Augsburg, the principle of "cuius regio, eius religio" was imposed, meaning that whatever the religious confession of the ruler was, so would be the religion of that territory. As a result, the Pope lost power in the Empire, and the princes gained strength. Karl V abdicated as Emperor in 1556.

This peace remained relatively stable, though tenuous, and lasted almost 70 years until the start of the Thirty Years' War in 1618.

Self-Evaluation

Celebrations and gifts

When listening, I can understand (Hören)

- Conversations on how to organize a party: *„Ja Mama, am 15. März machen wir unsere Geburtstagparty.“*
- Different people and conversations at a party: *„Weißt du, wenn Anna singt, muss ich weinen …“*

In written texts, I can understand (Lesen)

- Gift cards and opinions about them: *„Gutscheine sind kein Geschenk, finde ich. Ich kaufe lieber etwas.“*
- Simple e-mails and cards describing how a celebration went: *„Liebe Dörte, vielen Dank für deine E-Mail …“*
- Invitations to different celebrations: *Tanz auf dem Balkon*

I can produce the following oral structures (Sprechen)

- Talk about gifts and express ideas for gifts: *„Schenkst du deiner Mutter eine Handcreme?“*
- State requests
- Describe my impressions and experiences, for example: *über die Hochzeit eines Freundes*
- Express my opinion and convince others of something: *„Mir ist wichtig, dass die Musik …“*
- Recommending something to someone: *„Probier doch mal die Torte, die ist wirklich lecker!“*

I can produce the following written texts (Schreiben)

- Tell about a party in writing: *„Lieber …, stell dir vor: Am Wochenende war ich auf der Hochzeit von …“*
- A small poem: *„die Kette/für meine Frau/ich kaufe sie ihr/wie teuer“*.
- A response to an invitation: *„Danke für die Einladung. Endlich …“*

Answers to the XXL Exercises

Chapter 1

7 Translate into English.
a Why didn't you call me? – Because I didn't have your cell phone number.
b Julie works as an au pair because she likes to play with children.
c Peter fell asleep in class again. – How embarrassing!

8 Translate into German.
a Wie war die Reise? Erzähl mal! – Es war schrecklich! Warum? Was ist passiert? – Ich habe fast das Flugzeug verpasst und dann sind die Koffer nicht gekommen. – So ein Pech!
b Erklären Sie uns bitte nochmal die Übung? – Ich habe sie doch schon erklärt! – Ja, aber wir haben sie nicht verstanden.
c Mein Bruder ist schon 30 (Jahre alt), aber er wohnt noch bei meinen Eltern. – Arbeitet er denn nicht? – Doch, aber er verdient nicht viel und die Wohnungen sind sehr teuer.

9 Translate into German.
a Warum kommst du (denn) nicht mit? – Weil ich noch die Koffer auspacken muss. Und danach muss ich einkaufen.
b Ich bin heute nicht zum Training gegangen, weil ich so müde war. – Ja, aber am Mittwoch kannst du auch nicht (gehen), weil da Julias Geburtstag/der Geburtstag von Julia ist.
c Meine Cousine wohnt in Berlin. Sie heißt Francine und studiert Wirtschaft. Sie wohnt in einer Wohngemeinschaft (WG), zusammen mit zwei Polinnen/Mädchen aus Polen.

Chapter 2

4 Translate into English.
a Where are the garbage containers? – They're downstairs in the courtyard.
b I can't find my keys (I'm not finding my keys). – You set them down on the table.
c Put the bike behind the house. – Oh no, I'd rather take it in(to) the basement.
d The bottles belong in here, the paper goes there. – And where does plastic waste go?
e Can you all come over here? We can eat now. – Wait, we're coming right away.

5 Translate into German.
a Hast du mein Handy gesehen? – Ja, du hast es in deine Jacke gesteckt.
b Frau Söll, wohin haben Sie denn die CD-ROM gelegt? / Wo haben Sie denn die CD-ROM hingelegt? – Sie liegt auf Ihrem Tisch.
c Hier, leg die Fotos in den Schreibtisch. – Nein, ich möchte sie an die Wand hängen.

6 Summarize in German.
Wir sollen ein Zimmer reservieren, bei der Touristeninformation anrufen und Theaterkarten kaufen.

Chapter 3

5 Translate into English.
a That's Guido's computer, isn't it? – No, that's mine. His is back there.
b I forgot my book. – Here, you can take mine.
c Do you perhaps need a Gameboy? – No thanks. Our children already have one, and one is enough!

6 Translate into German.
a Gibst du mir bitte ein Glas? – (Ja,) hier/da hast du eins.
b Übrigens, haben wir noch Bananen? / Sind noch Bananen da? – Ja, wir haben/da sind noch welche. Möchtest du eine?
c Möchten Sie einen Kaffee? – Nein vielen Dank, ich möchte keinen.
d Ich finde meinen Stift nicht. Kann ich (mal) Ihren haben? – Ja, natürlich.

7 Translate into German.
a Meistens esse ich zum Frühstück Müsli. / Zum Frühstück esse ich meistens Müsli. – Trinken Sie keinen Kaffee? – Nein, fast nie.
b Wir sollten vielleicht ein bisschen wiederholen. Morgen möchte/will ich einen Test schreiben. – Wie schade! Können wir nicht lieber ein Spiel machen?
c Sie sind bestimmt müde. Die Fahrt war lang. Ich bringe Sie ins Hotel. – Nein, vielen Dank. Ich habe im Zug geschlafen.

Chapter 4

4 Translate into English.
a Mm! The ice cream is really delicious! You really should try it. – No, thanks, I prefer to eat fruit.
b You shouldn't shower for such a long time. Water is expensive. – I was only in the shower for five minutes!
c Tom came too late again today. – Maybe we should speak with him.
d So what would you like to eat? Pick something. – No, thanks. Right now, I really don't want to eat anything.
e Did someone forget their car keys? The building manager found some. – No, in our group, no one drives here.

5 Translate into German.
a Was sollen wir machen, wenn wir mit der Übung fertig sind? – Ihr könnt den Wortschatz von Lektion 3 wiederholen.
b Wenn Herr Miller anruft, machen Sie bitte einen Termin mit ihm aus, für Freitag um 12 (Uhr). – Am Freitag um 12 müssen Sie zum Arzt (gehen)!
c Was ist passiert? Warum kommst du nicht? – Ich hatte ein Problem mit dem Auto. Wenn ich um 10 (Uhr) nicht da bin, (dann) fangt bitte schon an.

6 Translate into German.
a Hat jemand meine Tasche gesehen? – Ja, du hast sie auf den Stuhl gestellt. – Es ist schrecklich, ich suche immer etwas / immer suche ich etwas!
b Ist jemand von der Deutschabteilung da? – Tut mir leid, im Moment ist niemand da. Soll ich etwas ausrichten?
c Können/Könnten Sie mich bitte mit Frau Weber verbinden? – Tut mir leid, Frau Weber ist heute nicht im Büro. Soll sie Sie zurückrufen? – Nein danke, ich rufe morgen noch einmal an.

Chapter 5

5 Translate into English.
a Don't get so upset! – I am upset! The bus didn't come again today!
b Pedro should move more. Recently, he's gotten a little fat. – Yeah, he should jog a little.
c What are you thinking about right now? – Vacation. I would like to go to Ecuador again this year. – Yeah, that was really beautiful.
d I'm interested in a golf class. I'm a beginner. Can you recommend something for me? – Yes, right now we have a great offer.

6 Translate into German.
a Wartet nicht auf mich. Ich muss mich noch umziehen. – Gut, wir sehen/uns dann bei Marta.
b Erinnern Sie sich an Herrn Wagner? – Ja, wir haben uns im Four Seasons Hotel in New York kennengelernt, nicht?
c Was machen Sie, wenn Sie sich nicht konzentrieren können? – Dann gehe ich gehe spazieren. / Ich gehe spazieren.
d Sonntags schlafen wir gern lange.
– Ach ja? Wir nicht, wir stehen immer früh auf.

Chapter 6

3 Translate into English.
a You really should do exercise 4! – Oh, we forgot that!
b Mr. Burli, didn't you want to go at 3 o'clock today?
– Yes, but I still have to finish the program.
c Do you think that someone can be successful in a profession with bad grades? – I'm certain of it!
d Do you think it's awful that Bob was held back/flunked? – I don't really think it's that awful, but his father is angry.

4 Translate into German.
a Meine Mutter wollte Lehrerin werden, aber sie durfte nicht studieren.
b Sollte Anna nicht diesen Excel-Kurs machen? – Ja, aber der war montags und mittwochs und da konnte sie nicht.
c Ich bin sehr froh, dass Tony eine Stelle bei Mercedes gefunden hat. – Ja, er hat Glück gehabt, aber er spricht auch gut Deutsch, nicht?
d Entschuldigung, ich wollte Sie etwas fragen: Haben Sie sich auch für den Kurs „Die Kunst des Flirtens“ angemeldet? – Ja, warum?
e Als Kind musste ich immer mein Zimmer aufräumen und beim Einkaufen helfen. – Ja, ich auch.

Chapter 7

4 Translate into English.
a Do you give your grandparents anything for their birthday ? – Not always.
b Do you think it's good if someone gives a gift card as a gift? – No, I think it's better if you choose something for the person.
c I'll take the wallet. – Yes, very well. Shall I wrap it as a gift?
d How does this stupid exercise go? – Wait, I'll show you.
e My, but these flowers are beautiful! Who did you get them from? / Who gave them to you? – (From) my husband. Our anniversary was yesterday (we had our anniversary yesterday).

5 Translate into German.
a Hör mal, Mary, könntest du mir 5 Euro leihen? Ich gebe sie dir morgen zurück. – Kein Problem.
b David, wir brauchen (mal) das Wörterbuch. – Wartet, ich gebe es euch gleich.
c Die Kette ist aber schön! Wer hat sie dir geschenkt? / Von wem hast du sie (bekommen)? – Eine Freundin hat sie mir geschenkt. / Die hat mir eine Freundin geschenkt.
d Könnten Sie mir bitte einen Kaffee bestellen? – Ich habe Ihnen schon einen bestellt.
e Soll ich Ihnen meine Adresse aufschreiben? – Nein danke, Sie haben sie mir schon gegeben.
f Herr Peters, ich habe gehört, dass Sie geheiratet haben!
– Ja, vor einer Woche. – Herzlichen Glückwunsch!

Lektion 1

A

1 a Sibylle fährt zum Flughafen. Ihr Freund Hisayuki kommt heute zu Besuch. b Sie wartet lange am Flughafen. Das Flugzeug hat Verspätung. c Sie ist glücklich. Sie trifft Hisayuki endlich wieder. d Hisayuki möchte zwei Monate in Deutschland bleiben. Er macht einen Deutschkurs.

2 b ... weil das Flugzeug Verspätung hat. c ... weil sie Hisayuki endlich wieder trifft. d ... weil er einen Deutschkurs macht.

3 b arbeitet c gefällt d arbeitet

4 b Weil ich gestern keine Zeit hatte. c Weil ich den Film schon kenne. d Weil er krank ist. e Weil wir unsere Freundin abholen.

5 a ▲ Warum? ↘
■ Weil meine Mutter Gebúrtstag hat. ↘

b ◆ Gehen wir morgen wírklich joggen? ↗
■ Warúm nicht? ↗
◆ Na já, → weil doch dein Béin wehtut. ↘

c ● Franziska kommt heute nicht zum Únterricht. ↘
▼ Warúm denn nicht? ↘
● Weil ihre Tochter kránk ist. ↘

d ■ Ich gehe nicht mit ins Kíno. ↘
● Weil dir der Fílm nicht gefällt → oder warúm nicht? ↘
■ Ganz éinfach, → weil ich kein Géld mehr habe. ↘

7 Weil ich noch so müde bin. – Weil ich zu wenig geschlafen habe. – Weil ich im Bett bleiben möchte. – Weil ich meine Kleider nicht aufräumen will. – Weil das Wetter so schlecht ist.

8 b Sie ist müde, weil sie zu wenig geschlafen hat. c Er ist sauer, weil Sandra nicht gekommen ist. d Er ist traurig, weil er Carla zwei Monate nicht sieht.

9 b ... weil sie gestern in Urlaub gefahren sind. c ... weil sie heute ins Restaurant gehen möchten. d ... weil ihre Freundin heute gekommen ist.

10 *Musterlösung*: ... weil meine Eltern mich am Wochenende besuchen und wir für Samstag schon Kinokarten haben. Paul hat leider auch keine Zeit, weil er gerade in Berlin ist und erst am Sonntag zurückkommt. Ich hoffe, du bist nicht traurig.

B

12

ge ... t

	er/es/sie	er/es/sie
baden	badet	hat gebadet
bringen	bringt	hat gebracht
danken	dankt	hat gedankt
dauern	dauert	hat gedauert
enden	endet	hat geendet
feiern	feiert	hat gefeiert
heiraten	heiratet	hat geheiratet
putzen	putzt	hat geputzt
rauchen	raucht	hat geraucht
schauen	schaut	hat geschaut
wissen	weiß	hat gewusst
zahlen	zahlt	hat gezahlt

ge ... en

	er/es/sie	er/es/sie
bitten	bittet	hat gebeten
fliegen	fliegt	ist geflogen
liegen	liegt	hat/ist gelegen
riechen	riecht	hat gerochen
sitzen	sitzt	hat/ist gesessen
stehen	steht	hat/ist gestanden

13 hat gelernt – hat getanzt – hat gesucht – ist gekommen – ist gereist – hat gearbeitet – hat gekocht – hat gegessen

14 ist ... abgeflogen – ist ... angekommen – habe ... abgeholt – ist ... eingeschlafen

15 b abgeholt c angerufen d gefahren e ausgepackt, aufgehängt f gegangen g aufgestanden

16 a ... sind ... aufgestanden b ... bin ... zurückgefahren c ... ist ... mitgekommen d ... ist ... abgefahren e ... habe ... angerufen f ... haben ... abgeholt g habe ... eingekauft h ... hat ... ausgepackt i ... hat ... aufgehängt

17 a Sie ist abgefahren. – Sie ist angekommen. b Sie ist aufgestanden. – Sie ist ins Bett gegangen. c Sie hat die Tür aufgemacht. – Sie hat die Tür zugemacht. d Sie ist ausgestiegen. – Sie ist eingestiegen. e Sie hat ausgepackt. – Sie hat eingepackt.

18 b gegessen c getrunken d gegangen e eingestiegen f gefahren g angekommen h angefangen i zurückgefahren

19 a aufgestanden b getrunken c angekommen d gearbeitet e gefahren f eingekauft g gekocht h angerufen i gegangen j eingeschlafen

20 *Musterlösung*: ... bin ich viel zu spät aufgestanden, dann bin ich schnell mit dem Taxi zum Flughafen gefahren. In Palma ist dann mein Koffer nicht angekommen und Diego, mein Freund, war nicht am Flughafen. Später habe ich ihn angerufen und schließlich hat er mich abgeholt. Am Abend sind wir dann ganz toll essen gegangen.

21 *Musterlösung*: ... getroffen. ... sind wir dann ausgestiegen und ich habe dich angerufen. Aber du warst nicht zu Hause. Dann sind wir beide zusammen etwas trinken gegangen und danach sind wir noch in eine Disko gefahren. Dort haben wir bis drei Uhr getanzt. Schließlich war ich um halb vier zu Hause und bin sofort eingeschlafen.

C

22 a Maria hat fast das Flugzeug verpasst. b Was ist denn passiert? c Der Bus hat ein Rad verloren. d Maria hat auf der Reise keinen Kaffee bekommen.

25 a verstanden b begonnen c besucht d bezahlt e diskutiert f vergessen g bestellt

26 bedeutet – begonnen – besichtigt – bezahlt – erklärt – erzählt – verkauft – verloren – verschickt – versucht

27 *Musterlösung*: a ... aufgestanden. Sie hat schnell den Koffer gepackt. Aber sie hat kein Taxi bekommen. Also ist sie zum Bahnhof gelaufen. Aber sie hat den Zug verpasst. b Nach seiner Ankunft hat er ein Taxi vom Flughafen ins Hotel genommen. Aber wo war sein Koffer? Er hat nachgedacht. Oje! Er hat seinen Koffer am Flughafen vergessen.

D

28 b Ist das Peters Onkel? c Ist das der Mann von Frau Tahy? d Ist das Tante Käthes Haus? e Ist das die Freundin von Otto? f Ist das Angelas Tochter?

29 a Schwiegervater ... Schwiegermutter b Tante c Onkel d Cousine e Cousin f Nichte g Neffe h Schwägerin i Schwager

30

der	die
Schwiegervater	Schwiegermutter
Onkel	Tante
Cousin	Cousine
Neffe	Nichte
Schwager	Schwägerin

31 Onkel – Cousin – Bruder – Enkelkind – Vater – Nichte – Neffe – Opa – Tante – Schwager

E

33 b der alleinerziehende Vater c die Kleinfamilie d der Single

34 a Das ist eine Gruppe von Leuten ... c 1 Linda – 2 Angelika – 3 Angelika – 4 Linda

Lektion 2

A

1 c hängt d steht e steht, liegt f liegt, hängt g liegt h hängt i steckt j steht

2 a liegt b Steckt, liegt c hängt d stehen e liegt f hängt g liegt

3 auf – hinter – in – neben – über – unter – vor – zwischen

4 die Katze – die Wand – der Tisch – das Sofa – der Stuhl – das Regal – die Jacke – der Schrank – das Bett – das Buch

5 b vor dem c zwischen den d an der e auf dem f neben der g unter dem h im i über dem j hinter dem k vor den

7 a 2 der Schreibtisch 3 der Stuhl 4 das Regal 5 der Schrank 6 die Lampe 7 die Katze 8 der Tisch 9 die Bücher 10 der Teppich 11 das Bild 12 das Fenster 13 der Fernseher 14 der Papierkorb 15 das Bild 16 die (Blumen)Vase 17 die Tasche 18 das Glas 19 die Hose 20 die Jacke

B

9 b ... auf dem Bett c ... an der Wand

10

	Wohin? Ich lege das Buch ...	Wo? Das Buch liegt ...	
a	x		auf den Tisch.
		x	auf dem Tisch.
b		x	auf dem Schreibtisch.
	x		auf den Schreibtisch.
c		x	neben dem Bett.
	x		neben das Bett.
d	x		in den Schrank.
		x	im Schrank.
e		x	unter dem Stuhl.
	x		unter den Stuhl.

11 b an die c neben das d in den e an die f ins g auf den h an die i unter den j auf den

12

neben dem Schrank	neben den Schrank
an der Wand	an die Wand
unter dem Fenster	unter das Fenster

14 b gestellt – steht c gehängt – hängt d gesteckt – steckt

15 b in das / ins – im c unter dem – Unter dem d zwischen die – zwischen den Kleidern e neben das – neben dem f in die Tasche – in der Tasche g vor dem – vor dem h in den Papierkorb – In den

C

16 b Sie geht ins Haus. – Sie geht rein. c Sie geht in den dritten Stock. – Sie geht rauf. d Sie geht in den Hof. – Sie geht runter. e Sie geht über die Straße. – Sie geht rüber.

17 b raus c rüber d runter e rauf

18 b Hier darf man nicht reingehen. c Hier darf man nicht rausgehen. d Hier darf man nicht raufgehen. e Hier darf man nicht rübergehen. f Hier darf man nicht rauffahren.

20 a 2 b 1 c 2 d 1 e 1 f 2

D

23 b Party d Hof, Hausmeister e Frau f Kinderwagen g Katze h Keller i Ordnung

24 a das Haus + die Nummer – das Haus + der Meister – das Dach + die Wohnung – das Fahrrad + der Keller – der Müll + der Container – der Müll + die Tonne b kaufen + das Haus – mieten + die Wohnung – parken + der Platz – wohnen + das Zimmer – schreiben + der Tisch

E

26 b Ich bin ungefähr um 7 Uhr zurück. c Ich bin von Freitag bis Sonntag nicht hier. d Ich muss unbedingt zur Uni fahren. e Ich bekomme bald einen wichtigen Brief. f Bitte ruf deine Eltern an. Es ist wichtig.

27 einen Anruf erwarten/bekommen – Strom verbrauchen/bekommen – einen Brief schreiben/erwarten/bekommen – eine Freundin erwarten/wecken – ein Fahrrad bekommen/ausleihen – Blumen gießen/bekommen/ausleihen

28 a 6 c 7 d 2 e 4 f 3 g 5

Lektion 3

A

1 b Zweimal im Monat schwimmen – das ist genug! – Ich gehe manchmal schwimmen. c Schwimmen? Dreimal im Jahr, das ist o.k.! – Ich gehen selten schwimmen. d Schwimmen, nein danke. – Ich gehe nie schwimmen.

2 a immer b selten – oft c oft – selten d nie

B

5 b welche c einen d eins e keins f eine

6 b welche c keins d einer e keine f eins g keine h keiner

7

Nominativ	maskulin der (Löffel)	neutral das (Messer)	feminin die (Gabel)	Plural die (Tassen)
Hier ist ...	einer	eins	eine	
Hier sind ...				
Tut mir leid, hier ist ...				
hier sind ...	keiner	keins	keine	keine
Akkusativ	den	das	die	die
Ja, ich brauche ...	einen	eins	eine	welche
Nein, ich brauche ...	keinen	keins	keine	keine

8 a Pfanne b Schüssel c Teller d Gabel

9 b eure c deine d ihren e ihren f sein g meine – meinen h unser

10 a meinen b Deine c Ihrs d meins e meiner

11 a einen – einer b eure – unsere c keine – eine d Ihrer e ihren f seins

12 *Musterlösung*: **A** deins **B** Sagen Sie, ist das Ihr Schlüssel? Nein, das ist nicht meiner. Ich habe meinen hier. **C** Ich habe mein Feuerzeug vergessen. Kann ich Ihres nehmen? Natürlich, nehmen Sie meins.

C

13 a **1** ein kleines Frühstück **2** ein Glas Tee, eine Brezel mit Butter **3** ein Stück Käsekuchen, ein Stück Schwarzwälder Kirschtorte, zwei Tassen Kaffee b Tisch 3

14 a ... Gern. Was darf ich Ihnen bringen? – Einen Apfelsaft, bitte. – Und was möchten Sie essen? – Ich nehme den Braten mit Kartoffeln. b Wir möchten bitte zahlen. – Zusammen oder getrennt? – Zusammen. – Das macht 13,60 €. – Stimmt so.
c Entschuldigung! – Ja bitte? – Ich habe einen Milchkaffee bestellt und keinen Espresso. – Oh, das tut mir leid. Ich bringe Ihnen sofort den Milchkaffee.

15 a Kann ich bitte bestellen? – Was möchten Sie trinken? b Können wir bitte bezahlen? – Zusammen oder getrennt? – Stimmt so. c Ja natürlich, bitte sehr. d Oh, das tut mir leid!

18 a Mein Freund heißt Klaus. Er ist groß und isst meistens sehr viel. Deshalb ist er auch ein bisschen dick. Er macht auch selten Sport. Fußball im Fernsehen findet er besser. b Du trinkst ja nur Mineralwasser und isst nur Brot. Was ist denn passiert? c Reisen ist mein Hobby. Das macht mir Spaß. Ich habe schon dreißig Städte besucht. d Hallo, Susanne. Du musst schnell nach Hause kommen, ich habe schon wieder meinen Schlüssel vergessen.

D

19 schnell – Bratwurst – Cola – billig – mit den Händen essen – Pommes Frites

20

	scharf	sauer	süß	fett	salzig
a Chili	x				
b Schweinebraten				x	(x)
c Kuchen			x		
d Zitrone		x			
e Wurst				x	(x)
f Eis			x		
g Essig		x			
h Pommes Frites				x	x
i Schokolade			x		
j Sauerkraut		x			

21 a Mahlzeiten b Gericht c Metzgerei d probieren e schneidet f Rezept

E

23 **A** Setzen Sie sich doch! **B** Möchten Sie noch einen Kuchen? – Der Kuchen ist wirklich lecker. – Können Sie mir das Rezept geben? **C** Kommen Sie gut nach Hause. – Ich muss leider wirklich nach Hause. – Und vielen Dank für die Einladung.

24 b Der Kuchen schmeckt mir! c Nehmt doch bitte Platz! d Ich danke Ihnen für die Einladung!

25 a Ach schade, aber wir fahren am Wochenende nach Berlin. b Vielen Dank, das ist sehr nett von Ihnen. – Das wäre doch nicht nötig gewesen. c Ja, gern. Sie schmeckt wirklich lecker. – Die Nachspeise ist wirklich sehr gut. Aber ich habe leider keinen Hunger mehr. d Ach, bleibt doch noch ein bisschen. – Schon? Schade. Dann kommt aber mal gut nach Hause.

26 a 1c **2** d **3** a **4** b **5** e

b *Musterlösung*: ... Der Wein hat auch nicht besonders gut geschmeckt. Die Freunde von Klaus sind alle langweilig gewesen, nur Axel hat die ganze Zeit mit mir gesprochen. Aber auch er ist furchtbar langweilig gewesen! Ich bin dann früh gegangen und habe lieber andere Freunde getroffen. Mit ihnen habe ich dann bis zwei Uhr morgens viel Spaß gehabt. ...

Lektion 4

A

1 a Sie sollten im Büro nicht so viel rauchen! b Sie sollten im Büro nicht privat telefonieren! c Sie sollten die Füße nicht auf den Schreibtisch legen!

2 b solltest – Bild 1 c sollten – Bild 2 d solltest – Bild 1 e solltet – Bild 3 f sollten – Bild 2 g solltest – Bild 1 h solltet – Bild 3

3 b Sie sollten abends spazieren gehen. c Wir sollten einen Handwerker anrufen. d Sie sollte einen Terminkalender kaufen. e Du solltest nicht so viel Süßes essen. f Sie sollten eine paar Tage im Bett bleiben.

B

4 a Bild 2 b Bild 1 c Bild 3

5 b Wenn das Wetter schön ist, (dann) fahre ich mit dem Fahrrad. c Wenn ich keine Zeit habe, nehme ich die U-Bahn. d Wenn ich mit dem Auto fahre, (dann) brauche ich zehn Minuten bis zum Büro.

7 a Wenn Sie abends nach Hause gehen, schalten Sie bitte Ihren Computer aus. b Wenn Sie mittags in die Kantine gehen, schließen Sie bitte das Büro ab. c Wenn Sie Kopfschmerzen haben, kann ich Ihnen Medikamente geben. d Wenn Sie Kaffee getrunken haben, spülen Sie Ihre Tasse bitte selbst. e Wenn ein deutscher Text zu schwierig ist, übersetzt Frau Albrecht ihn für Sie.

8 b Sprechen Sie bitte mit dem Hausmeister, wenn im Büro etwas kaputt ist. c Rufen Sie bitte an, wenn Sie morgens einmal später kommen. d Fragen Sie Ihre Kolleginnen, wenn Sie Büromaterial suchen. e Kommen Sie zu mir, wenn Sie noch Fragen haben.

9 a ... Ihre Arbeit fertig ist. b ... Frau Volb da ist. c ... wir Sie immer anrufen können. d ... kein anderer Termin möglich ist.

11 b in einer Fabrik etwas produzieren c eine Quittung schreiben d den Gästen Tee und Gebäck anbieten e zu viel Geld ausgeben f den Computer ausschalten

C

13 a noch nicht b schon – noch nicht – noch nicht

14 a niemand b etwas – nichts – etwas c etwas – nichts d jemand – niemand

15 b S: Firma Hens und Partner, Maurer, guten Tag.
A: Guten Tag, hier spricht Grahl. Könnten Sie mich bitte mit Frau Pauli verbinden?
S: Tut mir leid, Frau Pauli ist außer Haus. Kann ich ihr etwas ausrichten?
A: Nein, danke. Ist denn sonst noch jemand aus der Export-Abteilung da?
S: Nein, es ist gerade Mittagspause. Da ist im Moment niemand da.
A: Gut, dann versuche ich es später noch einmal. Könnten Sie mir noch die Durchwahl von Frau Pauli geben?
S: Ja, gerne, das ist die 301. Also 9602-301.
A: Vielen Dank. Auf Wiederhören, und einen schönen Tag noch.
S: Danke, gleichfalls.

16 *Musterlösung*: a ... einen Arzttermin und kommt später in die Arbeit. Viele Grüße, Amelie Blau. b Liebe Frau Schön, Herr Hein aus der Export-Abteilung hat angerufen, er muss den Termin am 21.9 absagen. Er bittet Sie um Rückruf. Er möchte dann einen neuen Termin vereinbaren. c Sehr geehrte Frau Sporer, Herr Hassos von der Berliner Zeitung hat angerufen. Er möchte gern einen Termin vereinbaren. Sie sollen ihn bitten zurückrufen. Viele Grüße Andreas Meier d Liebe Susanne, hast du Zeit nach der Arbeit? Wollen wir noch etwas zusammen unternehmen? Vielleicht ein Glas Wein trinken oder ins Kino gehen. Gruß Gerd

19 ich: nicht – Rechnung – Nachricht – ausrichten – mich – möchte – Licht – Milch ...
auch: noch – Buch – Nachricht – Koch – besuchen – Sprache ...

D/E

20 a **1** Nachhilfe geben – **2** Kinder betreuen – **3** Zeitungen austragen
b **1** falsch **2** richtig **3** falsch **4** falsch

21 **1** 269 Euro **2** Café Peterhof in der Schillerstraße **3** Abflug 14:55 Uhr, Ankunft 16:35 Uhr

Lektion 5

A

1 a mich b euch – uns c sich – mich d sich – sich

2

ich	konzentriere	mich	wir	konzentrieren	uns
du	konzentrierst	dich	ihr	konzentriert	euch
er / es / sie	konzentriert	sich	sie / Sie	konzentrieren	sich

3 **C** Sie ärgert ihren Bruder. **D** Sie ärgert sich. **E** Er zieht das Baby aus. **F** Er zieht sich aus. **G** Sie kämmt ihre Tochter. **H** Sie kämmt sich. **I** Er wäscht das Baby. **J** Er wäscht sich.

5 b Wascht euch jetzt! c Dusch dich endlich! d Kämm dich jetzt endlich! e Zieht euch jetzt an! f ... bewegt euch endlich!

6 b dich c sich d sich e uns f euch g sich

7 a **2** Ziehen Sie sich nicht zu warm an! **3** Duschen Sie sich warm und kalt! **4** Bewegen Sie sich mehr! **5** Rauchen Sie nicht so viel!
b **2** Sie sollten sich nicht zu warm anziehen. **3** Sie sollten sich warm und kalt duschen. **4** Sie sollten sich mehr bewegen. **5** Sie sollten nicht so viel rauchen.

8 b Er ärgert sich immer über seinen Bruder. c Sie zieht sich heute eine Hose an. d Er legt sich jeden Mittag ins Bett. e Ich ernähre mich ab heute gesund.

9 b Immer ärgert er sich über seinen Bruder. c Heute zieht sie sich eine Hose an. d Jeden Mittag legt er sich ins Bett. e Ab heute ernähre ich mich gesund.

11 a / b

Man kann gesund bleiben	wenn man		nicht so fett	isst.
Man kann gesund bleiben	wenn man	sich	nicht so viel	ärgert.
Man kann gesund bleiben	wenn man		mehr Sport	macht.
Man kann gesund bleiben	wenn man		viel Obst und Gemüse	isst.
Man kann gesund bleiben	wenn man	sich	kalt und warm	duscht.
Man kann gesund bleiben	wenn man	sich	nicht zu warm	anzieht.
Man kann gesund bleiben	wenn man	sich	oft	ausruht.
Man kann gesund bleiben	wenn man		viel spazieren	geht.

12 *Musterlösung*: ... und mich mehr bewegen. Ich möchte zum Beispiel viel öfter spazieren gehen. Ich möchte mich gesund ernähren, mit viel Obst und Gemüse. Ich möchte mich weniger ärgern und mich dafür mehr ausruhen. Ich möchte auch mehr Konzentrationsübungen machen. Und ich will endlich weniger rauchen!

B

13 b dich – für c sich – für d euch – für e uns – für f sich – für g sich – für

14 *Musterlösung*: b Wir interessieren uns für Gymnastik. – Wir mögen Gymnastik. – Wir machen gern/oft Gymnastik. c Meine Freunde interessieren sich für Bücher. – Meine Freunde lesen gern Bücher. d Maria interessiert sich für Musik. – Maria mag Musik. – Maria hört viel Musik. e Meine Freundin interessiert sich für Tennis. – Meine Freundin mag Tennis. – Meine Freundin spielt gern Tennis.

15 a Heute Abend kümmere ich mich um die Kinder. – Hast du Lust auf ein Stück Schokolade? – Ich bin mit meinem Auto nicht zufrieden. – Ich erinnere mich nicht mehr an diese Person. b Manchmal träume ich von einem Urlaub in der Sonne. – Warten Sie auch auf den Bus nach Wiesbaden? – Ich verabrede mich nachher mit Klaus, o.k.? – Meine Tochter freut sich schon so sehr auf ihren zehnten Geburtstag. c Sprichst du noch mit ihr? – Denkst du bitte an die Blumen! – Ich ärgere mich immer über mein Auto. – Morgen treffe ich mich mit ein paar Freunden. – Hat er sich schon wieder über das Essen beschwert?

16

mit	auf	an	über	von	um
sich verabreden	warten	denken	sich ärgern	träumen	sich kümmern
sprechen	sich freuen	sich erinnern	sich beschweren		
sich treffen	Lust haben				
zufrieden sein					

17 b Ich denke nie an seinen Geburtstag. c Heute habe ich keine Lust auf Gymnastik. d Ich freue mich sehr auf die Sommerferien.
18 b den Urlaub c einem Auto d das Abendessen e den Zug f die Arbeit
19 b an dich c an die d von dir e mit dir f um die g auf den h über mich i auf die
20 a an dich b mit dir – Mit mir c auf dich – Auf mich d von mir – von dir
21 B Sie ärgern sich über ihre Kinder. C Unsere Kinder freuen sich schon auf Weihnachten. D Er wartet auf seine Freundin. E Entschuldigung, kann ich mal kurz mit Ihnen sprechen? F Ich möchte mich mal wieder mit dir treffen.
25 a Reise b wichtig c braun d Halt! e Herr f Hose

C

27 b Woran – Daran c worüber – darüber d worauf – darauf
28 b woran – daran c worüber – darüber, *aber*: dafür
29 a Woran – Worauf – Worüber – Woran b Daran – Darauf – Darüber – Daran
30 dafür – wofür, darüber – worüber, daran – woran

D

31 b Tennis c Golf d Eishockey e Handball f Tischtennis g Fußball h Wandern i Gymnastik j Skifahren k Snowboardfahren l Tanzen m Segeln
32 b Dienstags geht Susi mit Heidi joggen. c Mittwochs geht Susi zur Gymnastik. d Donnerstags geht Susi zum Tanzkurs. e Freitags geht Susi zum Schwimmen. f Samstags geht Susi ins Fitness-Studio zur Aerobic. g Sonntags geht Susi zum Klettern.
33 b 2 c 6 d 7 e 1 f 5 g 3
34

Situation	1	2	3	4	5
Anzeige	h	x	b	e	d

E

35 a machen: einen Spaziergang machen, Urlaub machen, Gymnastik machen, eine Reise machen, eine Busfahrt machen, Lärm machen
b gehen: ins Fitness-Studio gehen, tanzen gehen, ins Schwimmbad gehen, spazieren gehen
c fahren: Ski fahren, mit dem Fahrrad fahren
d spielen: Eishockey spielen, Handball spielen
36 b 2 c 5 d 3 e 1
37 a 1 Anrede: Liebe Susi, liebe Lisa; 2 „Unterschrift": Hanna; 3 Adresse: susi-q@weg.web; lisa-m@hin.de
4 Gruß: Viele Grüße; 6 Text: tut mir …
b 6, 3, 5, 7, 2, 4, 1
c *Musterlösung:*
Liebe Hanna, danke für deine Mail! Sport ist für mich wirklich wichtig. Ich sitze so viel im Büro – da brauche ich den Sport einfach. Ich mache jeden Morgen Gymnastik, dann gehe ich noch montags und freitags ins Fitness-Studio. Wenn ich kann, gehe ich zu Fuß: Ich kaufe zum Beispiel immer zu Fuß ein. Am Wochenende gehe ich joggen. Kommst du einmal mit zum Joggen? Das tut dir bestimmt gut.
Viele liebe Grüße
Lisa

Lektion 6

A

1 b 2 c 2 d 2 e 1 f 1
2 b durfte c sollte d wollte e durfte
3 b konnte c durfte d musste e konnte f sollte
4 b Am Dienstag wollte er mit Erika Eis essen, aber er musste mit seinem Vater Mathe lernen. c Am Mittwoch sollte er mit seiner Mutter Englisch lernen, aber er wollte lieber Skateboard fahren. d Am Donnerstag wollte er mit Inge ins Kino gehen, aber er musste das Geschirr spülen. e Am Freitag wollte er Fußball spielen, aber er musste Zeitungen austragen.
5 b ihr c ihr d sie, Sie e du f sie, Sie
6

ich	wollte	konnte	sollte	durfte	musste
du	wolltest	konntest	solltest	durftest	musstest
er / sie / es	wollte	konnte	sollte	durfte	musste
wir	wollten	konnten	sollten	durften	mussten
ihr	wolltet	konntet	solltet	durftet	musstet
sie / Sie	wollten	konnten	sollten	durften	mussten

7 a wollte, musste b Wollten, durften – wollte, musste c durfte, konnte
8 Als Kind wollte Lars Fußballspieler werden. Als Jugendlicher musste er mit seinen Eltern in eine neue Stadt umziehen. Mit 16 Jahren wollte Lars eine Lehre zum Mechaniker machen, aber er durfte nicht. Er sollte eine Lehre als Exportkaufmann machen. Nach der Lehre wollte Lars Abitur machen. Mit 22 Jahren hat Lars Abitur gemacht und er durfte studieren. Als Erwachsener konnte er endlich als Mathematiker arbeiten.

B

10 b Ich finde, dass er zu wenig für die Schule lernt. c Ich bin sehr froh, dass ich in Berlin studieren kann. d Es tut mir sehr leid, dass du schon wieder krank bist.

11 **a** Ich finde **b** Es tut mir leid **c** Es ist wichtig **d** Ich bin froh / Ich bin glücklich

12 **b** ... ein gutes Zeugnis wichtig ist. **c** ... Englisch langweilig ist. **d** ... ich mehr Grammatik üben muss.

13 **a** ... ich studieren durfte. **b** ... eine gute Ausbildung wichtig ist. **c** ... du schlechte Noten im Zeugnis hast. **d** ... du fleißig bist. **e** ... du ein bisschen mehr lernen kannst. **f** ... unsere Kinder eine gute Schule besuchen können.

15 *Musterlösung*: **a** ... ich wenig zu tun habe. **b** ... ich frei habe. **c** ... oft nicht streng genug sind. **d** ... gute Noten in der Schule hat. **e** ... nicht genug lernst. **f** ... ich hier immer so viele Überstunden machen muss. **g** ... Sie Ihre Lohnsteuerkarte schon abgegeben haben? **h** ... der Bus Verspätung hatte. **i** ... ich den Kollegen helfen kann.

16 wenig, langweilig, unwichtig, wichtig, ich, endlich, richtig, natürlich, eilig, zwanzig, pünktlich

17 glücklich – lustig – traurig – freundlich – ruhig – höflich – ledig – eilig – selbstständig – schwierig – langweilig – günstig – billig

19 Wein – Bier – bald – Brot – Wecker

20 **b** w 3x b / **c** w 2x b 1x **d** w 1x b 2x **e** w 2x b 1x **f** w 2x b 1x

C

22 **a** falsch **b** richtig **c** richtig **d** richtig **e** falsch

23 *Musterlösung*: **A** Alexander findet, dass die Schule oft langweilig ist. Er denkt, dass die Lehrer weniger Hausaufgaben geben sollen. Auch findet er schlecht, dass es zu wenig Sportunterricht gibt. **B** Seine Mutter meint, dass die Lehrer streng sein sollten. Sie findet schlecht, dass es zu wenig Unterricht in den Fächern Kunst und Musik gibt. Außerdem denkt sie, dass die Noten nicht so wichtig sind. **C** Sein Opa glaubt, dass die Schule heute besser als früher ist. Zum Glück sind die Lehrer heute nicht mehr so streng. Er findet gut, dass die Schüler mehr in Partnerarbeit und in Gruppen zusammenarbeiten.

24 **a** Sport **b** Kindergarten **c** froh **d** Handwerk **e** Krippe

25 **a** 2 – 6 – 1 – 4 –3 – 5

b *Musterlösung*:

Liebe ...,

wie geht es dir? Ich habe lange nichts von dir gehört. Seit zwei Monaten mache ich einen Deutschkurs in Wien. Jeden Morgen freue ich mich auf die Schule, weil ich einen sehr netten und lustigen Lehrer habe. In meiner Heimat waren die Lehrer nicht so nett. Sie waren streng. Das finde ich nicht so gut. Denn man lernt eine Sprache leichter, wenn die Lehrer freundlich sind, oder? Im Unterricht sprechen wir auch viel Deutsch und machen häufig Gruppenarbeit. Das macht so viel Spaß! Wie war der Sprachunterricht in deiner Schule? Bitte schreib mir bald! Ich freue mich auf eine Antwort von dir.

Viele Grüße

Samira

26 *Musterlösung:*

... Wie schön, dass dir der Unterricht in Deutschland gefällt. Meine Schulzeit war eigentlich recht schön: Ich bin nur in eine kleine Schule in Bolu gegangen. Mein Lieblingsfach war Musik. Unser Musiklehrer war nämlich sehr lustig. Er hat immer Witze erzählt und lustige Lieder mit uns gesungen. Die anderen Lehrer waren nicht so nett, aber mir hat die Schule gefallen. Schreib mir bald wieder über deine Zeit in Deutschland.

Herzliche Grüße

...

D

27 Schule: die Grundschule, das Fach, das Abitur, die Gesamtschule, die Note; Arbeit: der Angestellte, der Arbeitnehmer, die Bewerbung, der Arbeitsplatz, die Lehre, der Lohn, der Auszubildende, die Kündigung

28 **b** eine Datei speichern **c** an einem Kurs teilnehmen **d** ein Angestellter sein **e** Lohn bekommen **f** sich für Politik interessieren **g** Recht haben **h** den Notarzt rufen

29 **a** Lehre **b** Einführung **c** Beratung **d** Kultur

30 **b** Voraussetzung **c** Angst **d** Ärger **e** Einführung **f** Erfahrung **g** Kontakt

32 **a** Hauptschule – Fachhochschule **b** **1** falsch **2** falsch **3** richtig **4** richtig

E

33 **a** 2 **b** 4 **c** 5 **d** 1 **e** 3 **f** 6

34 **A** Schauspieler **B** Flugbegleiterin/Stewardess **C** Ärztin

Lektion 7

A

1 **b** ... seiner Schwester ein Buch. **c** ... unseren Eltern eine Reise. **d** ... ihrem Bruder eine Eintrittskarte. **e** ... eurem Hund eine Wurst. **f** ... ihren Großeltern eine Einladung zum Essen.

2

	Bruder	Kind	Schwester	Eltern	
Das ist / sind	mein	mein	meine	meine	.
Ich sehe	meinen	mein	meine	meine	morgen.
Ich schenke	meinem	meinem	meiner	meinen	nichts!

Answers to the Workbook Exercises

3 b mir – dir c euch d ihnen e uns f ihr g ihm h ihnen
4 a 2 ein Fahrrad 3 ein Kochbuch 4 einen Fußball 5 ein Spiel 6 ein Computerspiel
b 2 ihr ein Fahrrad 3 ihm ein Kochbuch 4 ihnen einen Fußball 5 ihr ein Spiel 6 ihm ein Computerspiel
5 A helfen – passt – steht B schmeckt C gehören
6 b Ich bestelle mir einen Salat. c Meine Freundin bringt mir Blumen mit. d Sie schenkt ihrer Oma Schmuck. e Gibst du mir noch ein Stück Kuchen?
8 2 Steht 3 hilf 4 gefallen 5 wünsche 6 gehören 7 mitbringen 8 passen 9 schmeckt
11 Geburtstagsfest – Geburtstagsparty – Geburtstagskarte – Geburtstagsfeier – Geburtstagskuchen – Hochzeitstag – Hochzeitsfeier – Einkaufsbummel

B

13

	Ich kenne ...	Wer gibt ... zehn Euro?		Ich kenne ...	Wer gibt ... zehn Euro?
ich	mich	mir	**wir**	uns	uns
du	dich	dir	**ihr**	euch	euch
er	ihn	ihm	**sie / Sie**	sie / Sie	ihnen / Ihnen
es	es	ihm			
sie	sie	ihr			

14 b Hast du es deiner Schwester gegeben? c Können Sie ihn mir wirklich empfehlen? d Kannst du es mir leihen? e Ich schreibe sie dir auf. f Kannst du ihn mir bestellen?
15 b sie ihm c es uns d sie Ihnen e sie mir f sie dir
16 b ... Ihnen sehr empfehlen! c ... ihn Ihnen sehr empfehlen! d ... sie Ihnen sehr empfehlen.
17 *Musterlösung*: b Ich erkläre es dir. c ... es dir selbst kaufen. d ... gebe sie dir sofort. e ... hole ihn euch gleich. f ... bringe sie Ihnen.
18 a es b es c es d gebe ihn e ihn

C

20 b 2 Die Blumen hat sie von ihrem Sohn bekommen. 3 Den Wein hat sie von ihrem Chef bekommen. 4 Die Kette hat sie von ihrer Tochter bekommen. 5 Die Kaffeemaschine hat sie von ihrer Schwester bekommen. 6 Die Torte hat sie von ihren Nachbarn bekommen.

D

23

Bild	1	2	3	4	5	6
Satz	f	d	c	a	b	e

24 *Musterlösung*: ... Bernhard und Bianca haben die Ringe getauscht und ‚Ja' gesagt. Vor der Kirche haben dann viele Freunde und Bekannte auf sie gewartet. Dann sind das Brautpaar und alle Gäste (hupend) durch die Straßen zum Restaurant gefahren. Nach dem Hochzeitsessen hat das Brautpaar zuerst getanzt. Es war sehr lustig und am Ende haben alle getanzt. Dann hat die Braut den Brautstrauß geworfen und wir Mädchen mussten ihn fangen. Clara hat ihn gefangen! Das heißt, dass sie als Nächste heiratet. Es war wirklich ein tolles Fest! Schade, dass du nicht dabei sein konntest ...

E

26 b tanzen c unterhalten d kochen e organisieren f kaufen g einladen h passen i dekorieren
27 a A 2 B 1 C 3
b *Musterlösung*:
Liebe(r) ...,
vielen Dank für die Einladung. Ich freue mich schon auf das Fest. Kann ich ein paar Freunde aus Italien mitbringen? Sie besuchen mich über Silvester. Wir bringen Jacken und Mäntel mit. Können wir, wenn es zu kalt ist, auch im Haus feiern? Brauchst du noch etwas zu essen oder zu trinken? Ich bringe gerne etwas mit. Auch meine CDs kann ich mitbringen. Bitte melde dich noch einmal.

Test zu Lektion 1

1 a ..., weil ihre Katze krank ist. b ..., weil sie nach Österreich fahren möchte. c ..., weil sie einkaufen muss. d ..., weil sie Kinder mag.

2

Ich habe ...	Ich bin ...
begonnen	abgefahren
erzählt	mitgekommen
verpasst	
aufgeschrieben	

3 *Musterlösung:*
a Sie hat (mit ihrem Freund) telefoniert. b Sie hat (Lebensmittel) eingekauft. c Er hat geschlafen. d Er ist nach Neuss gefahren. e Er hat ferngesehen. f Er ist aufgestanden.

4 a Der Vater von meinem Mann ist mein Schwiegervater.
b Der Sohn von meinem Sohn ist mein Enkelkind.
c Die Schwester von meiner Frau ist meine Schwägerin.
d Der Bruder von meinem Bruder ist mein Bruder.
e Die Schwester von meinem Vater ist meine Tante.
f Die Tochter von meiner Schwester ist meine Nichte.

5 *Musterlösung*:
Heute war wirklich ein schrecklicher Tag. Zuerst bin ich zu spät aufgestanden. Dann bin ich in den falschen Bus eingestiegen und in die falsche Stadt gefahren. An der nächsten Haltestelle bin ich wieder ausgestiegen.
Zwei Stunden später war ich wieder zu Hause. Dann habe ich mich vollkommen fertig auf das Sofa gelegt.
Schließlich bin ich wieder eingeschlafen und habe meinen Deutschkurs verpasst.

Test zu Lektion 2

1 a am b am c im d Im e auf dem f an die g auf den

2 a Die Zeitung steckt in der Tasche. b Die Bücher liegen im Regal. c Die Zeitung steckt im Briefkasten. d Die Frau stellt die Fotos auf den Tisch. e Die Kleider hängen im Schrank.

3 a rauf b runter c rüber

4 a richtig b falsch c falsch d falsch e falsch

5 *Musterlösung:*
Liebe Anna! Ich muss heute eigentlich die Wohnung putzen, aber leider bin ich heute den ganzen Tag an der Uni! Ich habe einfach keine Zeit. Könntest du das heute machen? Das Bad und die Küche ... ? Würdest du bitte auch beim Vermieter anrufen, weil doch das Küchenfenster nicht mehr richtig schließt? Und sei doch bitte so nett und gieße auch die Blumen und füttere meine Lola? Ich habe das leider auch vergessen. Hoffentlich ist das alles in Ordnung! Du musst jetzt alles ganz alleine machen. Ich hoffe, wir sehen uns heute Abend. Dann koche ich für uns. Danke für deine Hilfe!
Liebe Grüße
...

Test zu Lektion 3

1 a nie b oft c selten / manchmal d meistens / fast immer e nie f manchmal / selten

2 a Ich brauche einen großen Topf. Manfred, bringst du mir bitte einen? b Ich brauche eine Schüssel. Klara, bringst du mir bitte eine? c Dazu brauche ich ein Messer. Marion, gibst du mir bitte eins? d Kaufst du bitte welche? e Ich brauche einen Bierkrug. Holst du mir bitte einen? f Tina, holst du uns bitte welche?

3 2 c 3 e 4 a 5 b 6 f 7 g

4 *Musterlösung:*

Bild A:

Tina: Hallo, schön, dass ihr da seid!
Marie + Robert: Hallo! Wir haben dir ein paar Blumen für deine neue Wohnung mitgebracht.
Tina: Die sind aber schön, vielen Dank! Kommt doch rein, ich habe schon Kaffee gemacht.
Marie: Das ist aber nett. Wie geht es dir denn?
Tina: Gut, danke.

Bild B:

Robert: Hmm, der Kuchen schmeckt aber lecker, hast du den selbst gebacken?
Tina: Ja, das ist ein Rezept von meiner Oma. Den habe ich als Kind schon sehr gern gegessen.
Marie: Vielleicht kannst du es uns ja aufschreiben, dann kann ich es auch einmal ausprobieren.
Tina: Möchtest du noch ein Stückchen, Robert?
Robert: Ja, sehr gerne.

Test zu Lektion 4

1 a Sie sollten in die Kantine gehen, wenn Sie Hunger haben. b Ihr solltet jeden Tag Zeitung lesen! c Du solltest nicht so viel fernsehen! d Du solltest nicht so viele Überstunden machen! e Ihr solltet nicht dauernd streiten!

2 *Musterlösung:*
a Dann solltest du die Mietanzeigen lesen. b Dann sollte er Bewerbungen schreiben. c Dann solltest du Urlaub nehmen. d Dann solltest du einen Kurs machen.

3 a Wenn die Brezeln zu teuer sind, kaufen die Leute sie nicht beim Bäcker. b Wenn Herr Keller eine Arbeit braucht, muss er eine Bewerbung schreiben. c Wenn du Berufsanfänger bist, solltest du im Büro nicht privat

telefonieren. d Wenn die Kunden in der Apotheke nett sind, freut sich Susanne. e Wenn Paul später ins Büro kommt, muss er am Empfang anrufen.

4 a Nein, für dich hat niemand angerufen. b Nein danke, ich möchte nichts trinken. c Nein, ich habe ihr noch nicht gratuliert. d Nein, ich brauche nichts aus der Stadt. e Nein, ich habe noch nicht mit ihr gesprochen.

5 *Musterlösung*:
Liebe Maja,
gerade hat ein Herr Wunderlich angerufen. Er sagt, er braucht mehr Informationen über das Produktangebot. Könntest du ihn bitte zurückrufen? Die Nummer ist ...
Lieben Gruß
...

Test zu Lektion 5

1 a Er zieht sich aus. b Die Frau kämmt das Mädchen. c Der Vater zieht sein / das Kind an. d Er wäscht sich. e Er kämmt seine / die Kinder. f Sie kämmt sich.

2 a euch b sich c dich d sich e mich f euch

3 b 8 c 1 d 9 e 4 f 3 g 5 h 2 i 7

4 a Wofür b Worauf c Worüber d Worauf e Wovon

5 *Musterlösung:*
a Ich interessiere mich für Musik. b Ich habe nie Lust auf Sport. c Ich ärgere mich oft über meine Eltern. d Ich freue mich auf meinen Urlaub. e Ich habe heute von meinem Freund geträumt.

Test zu Lektion 6

1 a Petra wollte Lehrerin werden. Aber sie durfte die Schule in der Stadt nicht besuchen. Sie musste auf dem Bauernhof helfen. b Mein Bruder und ich wollten zusammen einen Bus kaufen. Aber wir hatten kein Geld. c Konntest du mit vier Jahren schon lesen? d Als Kinder durften wir nie allein in den Wald gehen. e Ich konnte noch nie gut rechnen. f Die Kinder mussten am Samstag immer das Auto waschen. Der Vater wollte das so.

2 a Es tut mir leid, ... b Es ist wichtig, ... c Ich bin froh, ... d Ich glaube, ... e Ich weiß, ...

3 a ..., dass er nicht in die Schule will. b ..., dass sie immer eine gute Schülerin war. c ..., dass die Kinder ihre Hausaufgaben machen müssen. d ..., dass sie ihren Sportlehrer liebt.

4 a Gesamtschule b Grundschule c Gymnasium d Universität

5 A3; B1; C2

6 a Kindergarten b Lieblingsfach c Zeugnis d sitzen bleiben e Beruf

Test zu Lektion 7

1 *Musterlösung:*
a Du schenkst deinem Vater einen Computer. b Wir schenken unseren Kindern Fahrräder. c Ihr schenkt eurer Freundin eine Puppe. d Ich kaufe meiner Schwester ein Bild. e Petra leiht ihrer Mutter eine CD.

2 a den b der c dem d dem e dem f den

3 a Nein, ich leihe es ihm nicht. b Nein, ich kann es euch nicht leihen. c Ich habe es ihnen schon gestern gegeben. d Ich bringe sie dir.

4 B7; C1; D2; E6; F3; G5